PRESSURE CANNING COOKBOOK FOR BEGINNERS

1200 Days of Easy Homemade Recipes to Keep Your Pantry Always Stocked. Meat, Fish, Beans, Soups, Vegetables, and Fruits Ready to Taste All Year Round

Allison Lawrence

Table of Contents

INTRODUCTION 9
CANNING 10
  CHAPTER 1: FRUITS 13
   1. Brandied Honey and Spice Pears 13
   2. Honey-Lavender Peaches 14
   3. Honey and Cinnamon Peaches 14
   4. Honey-Lavender Peaches .... **Errore. Il segnalibro non è definito.**
   5. Spiced Apple Rings 14
   6. Pickled Plums 15
   7. Spicy Ginger Red Hot Pears 15
   8. Caramel Apple Butter 15
   9. Port and Cinnamon Plums 16
   10. Apple Jam 16
   11. Green Tea Spiced Peaches 16
  CHAPTER 2: VEGETABLES 18
   12. Asparagus Spear 18
   13. Tomato Ketchup 18
   14. Carrots 19
   15. Tomatoes 19
   16. Herbed Tomatoes 19
   17. Asparagus 20
   18. Marinated Mushrooms 20
   19. Herbed Peas 20
   20. Cabbage with Beans 20
   21. Asparagus Spears 21
   22. Corn Kernel 21
   23. White Potatoes 21
   24. Tomatoes—Whole 22
   25. Canned Asparagus 22
   26. Canned Plain Beets 22
   27. Hot Peppers 22
   28. Canned Kale 23
   29. Sweet Peppers 23
   30. Canned Turnips 23
   31. Caramelized Onions 24
   32. Fiddleheads 24
   33. Glazed Carrots 24
   34. Canned Carrots 25
   35. Canned Potatoes 25
   36. Canned Sweet Potatoes 25
   37. Pressure Canned Tomatoes 26
   38. Shelled Lima Beans 26
   39. Canned Broccoli 26
   40. Blue Ribbon Green Beans 26
   41. Canned Parsnips 27
   42. Canned Succotash 27
  CHAPTER 3: MEAT, SEAFOOD AND POULTRY 28
   43. Hearty Chili 28
   44. Canned Tuna 29
   45. Minced Clams 29
   46. Canned Shrimp 29
   47. Pot Roast in a Jar 30
   48. Canned Ground Beef 30
   49. Chipotle Beef 30
   50. Canned Goulash 31
   51. Canned Chicken and Gravy 31
   52. Canned Meatballs 31
   53. Canned Pork 32
   54. Canned Turkey 32
   55. Ground Beef and Cabbage Soup ... 32
   56. Homemade Canned Pork 33
   57. Canned Beef Stroganoff 33

58. Canned Chili 33
59. Ground Beef, Pork, Lamb, or Sausage 34
60. Meat Stock 34
61. Chili with Beef 34
62. Beef in Wine Sauce 35
63. Beef Meatballs 35
64. Ham 35
65. Ground Beef in Tomato Sauce 36
66. Canned Venison 36
67. Smoky Meatloaf 37
68. Chicken Soup 37
69. Canned Chicken 37
70. Mexican Turkey Soup 38
71. Pineapple Chicken 38
72. Chicken Breast 38
73. Rosemary Chicken 39
74. Canned Turkey Pieces 39
75. Turkey and Green Beans 39
76. Turkey Sausage 39
77. Chili with Beef (2nd Version) 40
78. Chicken with Garlic 40
79. Venison 41
80. Canned Roast Beef 41
81. Chicken Soup 41
82. Canned Lamb 41
83. Beef Stroganoff with Mushroom 42
84. Canned Tilapia 42
85. Canned Chicken Pieces 42
86. Canned Turkey Meat 43
87. Canned Chili 43
88. Chicken Jambalaya with Sausage 43
89. Crumb Meatballs with Sauce 44
90. Stewing Beef 44
91. Pressure Canned Fish 44
92. Beef, Lamb, and Venison 45
93. Buttered Chicken Breast 45
94. Canned Whole Clams 46
95. Canned Shad Fish 46
96. Chicken and Potato 46
97. Canned Beef Cubes 47
98. Canned Chili Beans and Beef 47
99. Canned Chicken in a Jars 47
100. Fish Chowder 48
101. Fish Rice Casserole 48
102. Canned Oysters 48
103. Canned Trout 49
104. Minced Clams 49
105. Canned Mackerel 49
106. Canned Salmon 49

CHAPTER 4: BEANS AND LEGUMES . 51
107. White Beans 51
108. Chickpeas 52
109. Pinto Beans Chili 52
110. Kidney Beans Chili 52
111. White Beans and Corn Chili 53
112. Black-Eyed Peas 53
113. Red Lentils 54
114. Corn 54
115. Sweet and Sour Beans 54
116. Baked Beans 55

CHAPTER 5: SOUPS, STEW, SAUCES, AND BROTH 56
117. Beef & Potato Stew 56
118. Beef Broth 56
119. Mexican Beef and Sweet Potato Soup 57
120. Veggie Stew 57

121. Chicken Broth 57
122. Asparagus Soup 58
123. Potato and Leek Soup 58
124. Veggie Soup 59
125. Fennel and Carrot Soup 59
126. Chicken Soup 59
127. Beef Stew with Vegetables 60
128. Five-Bean Medley 60
129. Vegetable Soup 60
130. Aztec Chicken Soup 61
131. Black Bean Soup 61
132. Black Eyed-Pea Soup 62
133. Butter Squash Soup 62
134. Carrot and Fennel Soup 62
135. French Onion Soup 63
136. Beef Bone Broth 63
137. Chicken Bone Broth 64
138. Chicken Stock 64
139. Spicy Roasted Pork Broth 65
140. Creole Sauce 65
141. Mango BBQ Sauce 65

CHAPTER 6: BONUS RECIPES 67
142. Balsamic Tomato Jam 67
143. Ginger Nectarine Jam 67
144. Ground Turkey Taco Salad 67
145. Fig & Pistachio Jam 68
146. Dehydrated Candied Bacon 68
147. Soy Marinated Salmon Jerky 68
148. Teriyaki Beef Jerky 68
149. Mango Jalapeño Jam 69
150. Split Pea Soup 69
151. Onion Jam 69
152. Jalapeno Fish 70
153. Red Pepper Jam 70

154. Banana & Pineapple Butter 70
155. Soft Cheese 71
156. Peachy Rum Conserve 71
157. Spiced Pear Butter 71
158. Rhubarb Compote with Ginger 72
159. Kale Slaw 72
160. Lemon-Lime-Orange Marmalade 72
161. Apricot Amaretto Jam 73
162. Balsamic Vinegar-Ruby Port Jelly
  73
163. Jasmine Tea Jelly 73
164. Vanilla Pear Berry Jam 74
165. Apple Pie Jam 74
166. Peach Mango Jam 74
167. Honey Blueberry Cobbler Jam 75
168. Cherry Jam 75
169. Mango Jam 75
170. Pineapple Jam 75
171. Lemon Ginger Marmalade 76
172. Peach Butter 76
173. Beef Stew 76
174. Pears 77
175. African Curry 77
176. Simple Tomato Sauce 77
177. Greek Peas with Tomato and Dill 78
178. Bottled Spaghetti Sauce 78
179. Raspberry Peach Jam 78
180. Tri-Berry Jam 79
181. Pineapple Chipotle 79
182. Green Salsa 79
183. Red Pepper Marmalade 79
184. Tart Berry Apple Butter 80
185. Tropical Fruit Butter 80
186. Caramel Apple Butter 80

187. Pickled Blueberries 80
188. Southern Pickled Peaches 81
189. Pickled Green Beans 81
190. Watermelon Pickles 81
191. Pickled Radish 82
192. Pickled Mostaccioli 82

Conversion Tables............................83

INTRODUCTION

Canning is a method that allows the flavor of fresh and delicious products to be enjoyed year-round and it is the easiest way to keep preserves tasting great and fresh, while protecting against bacteria. Canning at home is a relatively straightforward process, and is a great solution for anyone hoping to create preserves to be enjoyed down the road.

Canning the Product

Once the preserves have been created, the product can be placed in the jars used to hold it. After boiling down the preserves, any foam on the top of the product should be removed. Preserves can then be poured into the containers. Many canners use a funnel to make this step a bit easier, eliminating the potential for waste in the process. About 1/4 inch of space should be left between the lip of the jar and the preserves. The cans and the lids need to be warm to complete this process. Many choose to use their dishwashers to heat jars to a suitable temperature. Lids can be placed in a small saucepan of simmering water until ready. Once the hot jars have been filled with preserves, the lids can be retrieved from the water and placed on top of the jar. The rings can then be added, tightening against the lids until snug. Filled jars with their lids are then placed in a canner, where they will be boiling for about 10 minutes. The exact method differs from canner to canner.

Canning without a Canner

Canning preserves used to do without the use of a canner. Unfortunately, there is a high risk for bacteria and food borne illnesses to occur when prepared without one of these devices. Because of this, it is important to utilize a canner to ensure that jars are correctly sterilized and the product inside remains safe to eat. Canning is a pastime that has been enjoyed for centuries. When performed effectively, canned goods can be saved in a cool, dry place for many months. Many canners make large batches of preserves when foods are in season, in turn savoring these delicious mixtures throughout the year. Learn how to can your own preserves at home and have these available for easy use, you will love our directions on how to make it happen. Learn how to keep food fresh from spoiling through different types of canning. We have included 1200 days of easy and inexpensive recipes so you can get started right away. Enjoy!

CANNING

Canning is a time honored, proven way of preserving a harvest or hunt for a very long time. In the course of a day, one can "put up" enough tomatoes (or other items) to last until the following year's harvest. However, all instructions must be followed completely to prevent illness or injury during the process. There are no shortcuts when preserving food, no matter which method is used. Let us start with a brief description of how and why canning preserves food. To maintain food, microbial growth and enzymatic changes must be halted or eliminated altogether. In canning, food is brought to a boil for a specified period to sterilize it. It is then packed into sterile jars, and sealed with sterile lids. Stopping here would keep the food edible for only a short period. You might be asking how, if everything has been properly sterilized, any microbe would exist to spoil what you have so carefully prepared. What is in the jars? Your carefully prepared food is there, yes; but also there is air – non-sterile air, to be exact. How do we get rid of the air? If the food is acid enough, it can process in an open water bath. Boiling does not kill the spores of the botulism bacteria (Ciostridium botuiinum); however, the high acid prevents these spores from growing. The hot, sealed jars are set on a rack and placed in a kettle of boiling water for a set period.

The water must keep at a brisk boil the entire processing time. Should the water fall below the boiling point, it must bring back up to boiling and the processing time starts over. In addition, the level of the boiling water must be kept at least an inch deeper than the height of the jars (do not mix jar sizes in the batch). This process is sufficient for driving the air out of the jars. After the processing time is complete, the jars are removed from the water, the rings or lids tightened as needed, and set on wire racks to cool. Almost immediately, you will hear that satisfying "pop" of the lids concaving, showing that a vacuum has indeed been created in the jars. After jars have cooled, test each one by pressing on the center of the lid. If it flexes when you push down, it is not sealed. Any vacuum-sealed jar must be reprocessed or refrigerated and eaten within a few days.

Pressure canning is necessary for foods that do not contain a high enough acid to prohibit the growth of botulism spores. While the temperature of boiling water (212°F) is not high enough to kill this bacteria's spores, pressure canners can increase the temperature to 240°F, holding it there long enough to kill them completely. Two to three inches of water were brought to a simmer in the canner. Using the same preparation as water bath canning, hot, sterile food is packed into hot, sterile jars, and sterile lids put in place. The jars are then placed on a rack in the canner. Fasten the canner's lid into place, but do not set the weight on the vent or close the petcock (depending on which your canner uses). Turn up the heat to the highest setting and allow the water to come to a boil and stem to flow from the open vent/petcock in the shape of a funnel. Allow this steam to exhaust for ten minutes (use a timer!). After this time is up, close the petcock or set the weight over the vent. Pressure will now begin to build. If your canner has a pressure gauge (my personal preference), allow the pressure to increase quickly to eight pounds. Turn the heat down slightly, allowing the pressure to increase to the desired level. If there is no gauge, do not reduce the heat until the weight begins to jiggle and rock. Processing time begins now. You will probably need to adjust the heat a few times to keep the pressure constant at the desired level. When the amount of time needed has passed (again, use a timer), turn off the heat and allow the canner to depressurize on of its own volition. The time it takes for pressure to fall is needed for proper processing. Do not try to speed this process up in any way. Forced cooling can lead to contamination of the food. Forcing the canner open before the pressure has been resolved can lead to severe injury by steam and projectiles. After depressurization, and before the canner is completely cool, open the lid, lift out the jars, placing them on a wire rack and tighten the rings if needed. You will quickly learn to enjoy the music of lids popping into the concave position, proving your success. Test each jar for the correct seal, as instructed above. Using separate lids and rings may remove the rings once the jars have cooled and the seals have proven. Gently unscrew the ring and set it aside for your next batch.

Admire product of your hard work and then store the jars in a cool, dark place. Whether your recipe calls for the food to be hot or cold, it must be packed loosely, and boiling water poured into the jar to eliminate air pockets. Jars are never filled to the brim. Food swells during processing. If it oozes out of the jar, it can prevent the lid from sealing securely to the jar. If the jar is not packed with enough food and water, too much air-filled space is left and the air is not completely exhausted during the processing time. Either event will allow spoilage to occur. This space is called "headspace". The amount needed is specified in each recipe and needs to adhere. Use a ruler to ensure you have it correctly.

Work surfaces, tools, utensils, and equipment must all be clean (in some cases, sterile) and in good condition. If pressure canning, the lid's gasket (rubber seal) and rubber safety valve cover must be of the correct size (check for stretching or shrinking), have no cracks, and must be inserted into the lid and seated correctly. Follow the instructions provided by the manufacturer.

Pressure canners are sturdy vessels made of cast aluminum or stainless steel. They can last multiple lifetimes if properly cared for. If you received your pressure canner without instructions, as can happen with hand-me-downs, you can usually find them online. Begin this search by looking for a website for the manufacturer. It might take a little digging to find, but most are there. If not, there are websites devoted to only instruction and owner's manuals available in PDF formats, usually for no cost. Should you need to replace the gasket, these are readily available in most places that sell the cooker. If you have difficulty finding the one you need, they can order online. These items are inexpensive, at the time of this writing, they are generally around $10 (US).

They are frequently sold in a kit that includes the rubber stopper for the safety valve. This is because if the safety valve has been blown, it and the gasket need to be replaced before using the canner. Also, find out the reason it blew out and avoid making that mistake again. After interviewing several canners, and in my own experience, I have never heard of a "blow out". Nevertheless, I was always reminded to follow instructions carefully. Jars must be manufactured for the canning process. These jars are properly tempered for the extremes in temperature and pressure they will be placed. Never use old peanut butter or commercial jelly jars. Your jars should be free of cracks and chips. If using rings and lids, the rings should be round and screwed onto the jars easily. Lids with a rubber-like seal embossed onto it, are meant to be used only once. Never reuse last year's lids. Lids should not be dented. Remember, you are trying to produce not only an airtight, watertight seal, but also a vacuum in the jar. The seal must be sturdy enough to maintain this vacuum. If using jars with rubber rings and bails clamping the lid into place, these too must be in good condition. The ring must have no cracks and must be of the correct size, covering the entire rim of the jar.

Separate lids and seals nearly disappeared from the marketplace; however, they are now making a comeback. If using these, careful inspection should be made of each item to be sure it is in serviceable condition. Also coming back are screw-on lids that require no separate ring. However, like the flat lids, they are embossed with a seal. While very handy to use at the time, they are not reusable. Recipes are also to be followed carefully. Some seasonings can be adjusted to taste, salt, sugar, vinegar, or alcohol should measure accurately. These are the anti-microbial elements that ensure your product is safe for consumption.

CHAPTER 1: FRUITS

1. Brandied Honey and Spice Pears
Preparation Time: 15 minutes **Cooking Time: 5 minutes**
Servings: 6

Ingredients:
- 6 lb. sliced pears
- Ascorbic acid color keeper
- 4 cups apple juice, cranberry juice, or apple cider
- ½ cup lemon juice
- 1 ½ cups honey
- 3 tbsps. crystallized ginger
- 8 inches stick cinnamon, break the sticks into halves
- ½ tbsps. whole cloves
- ¼-cup brandy

Directions: Put the pear slices in the ascorbic acid to prevent the pears from discoloring. Set aside.
Make syrup in a 6–8-quart pot by combining apple juice, lemon juice, honey, ginger, cinnamon, and cloves. Boil while constantly stirring. Reduce the heat to low.
Drain the peas and put them to the syrup. Stir in brandy, then increase the heat until the mixture is boiling. Reduce the heat once more and simmer while occasionally stirring for 5 minutes or until the peas are almost tender.
Use a slotted spoon to pack the spears into clean pint canning jars, ensuring you leave a half-inch headspace. Spoon the syrup over the pears and maintain the half-inch headspace. Use a clean towel to wipe the pint jar rims and put the lids on.
Load the jars into the pressure canner and process them at 10 pounds of pressure.

Nutrition: Calories: 59.8; Carbs: 15.7g; Fat: 0g; Protein: 0g

2. Honey-Lavender Peaches

Preparation Time: 10 minutes
Canning Time: 70 minutes

Cooking Time: 10 minutes
Serving: 12

Ingredients:
- 15 pounds ripe peaches
- 4 cups water
- 1 ¾ cups honey
- 2/3 cup Riesling
- 1 tablespoon lavender buds, dried
- ½ tablespoon salt
- 1 lemon

Directions: Bring a large pot of water to boiling. Cook the peaches, in batches, in the boiling water for 60 seconds or until the skin starts to peel.
Use a slotted spoon for removing the peaches from the hot water and place them in a large bowl of ice-cold water. Peel the peaches after removing them from the cold water.
Remove the pits and cut them in half lengthwise.
Make the syrup by combining 4 cups of water, honey, Riesling, lavender buds, and salt in a large saucepan.
Cook over medium-high heat as you stir until the honey has all dissolved.
Cut 3 inches strips of lemon peel using a vegetable peeler. Reserve the lemon for other use.
Pack the peaches in the jars with the cut side facing down. Add the lemon peel, then spoon the syrup evenly among the jars leaving a ½-inch headspace.
Rinse the jar rims and place the lids and rings on the jars. Transfer the jars to the pressure canner and process at 10 pounds of pressure for 70 minutes.
Let the canner rest to cool before removing the jars and placing them on a rack to cool.

Nutrition: Calories: 539.8; Fat: 7.9g; Fiber: 1.8g; Carbs: 7.9g; Protein: 67.2g

3. Honey and Cinnamon Peaches

Preparation Time: 15 minutes
Servings: 7 pints

Cooking Time: 32 minutes

Ingredients:
- 3 lb. ripe peaches
- 1 cup honey
- 7 cinnamon sticks

Directions: Peel the peaches and dunk them in boiling water for 2 minutes. The skin will then come off.
Meanwhile, mix 9 cups of water and honey, and bring the mixture to a boil over medium heat.
Place a cinnamon stick in each sterilized pint jar. Pack the peaches in the jars and add the honey mixture, leaving some space. Clean the jar rims and adjust the lids.
Transfer the jars in the pressure canner with water so that the jars are covered by water at least 2 inches.
Cover the pressure canner with an ordinary lid that fits well and process the pint jars for 30 minutes in the boiling water.

Nutrition: Calories: 69.8; Carbs: 16.9g; Fat: 0g; Protein: 0g

4. Spiced Apple Rings

Preparation Time: 15 minutes
Servings: 8 pints

Cooking Time: 48 minutes

Ingredients:
- 12 lb. green apples
- 8 cups white sugar
- 6 cups water
- 1¼ cups white vinegar
- 3 tbsps. of whole cloves
- 8 cinnamon sticks

Directions: Wash, core, peel, and slice apples. The thickness needs to be small-medium to fit into the jar. In a large saucepan, combine sugar, water, vinegar, cloves, and cinnamon sticks.
Boil as you stir until sugar is dissolved. Then lower the heat and let simmer for 3 minutes. Add the apples to the saucepan, and cook for about 5 minutes.
Place the apples and syrup into the jars equally.
Process pint or quart jars at 10 pounds for 45 minutes for the weighted gauge of the pressure canner or 11 pounds if the pressure canner has a dial gauge.
Remove jars and let cool until at room temperature before storing. This may take about a day.

Nutrition: Calories: 34.8; Carbs: 8.7g; Fat: 0g; Protein: 0g

5. Pickled Plums

Preparation Time: 35 minutes **Cooking Time:** 60 minutes
Servings: 5 pints

Ingredients:

- 3-1/2 lb. red/ green or purple plums
- 2 onions
- 2 cups water
- 2 cups red wine vinegar
- 2-1/2 cups sugar
- 3 inches cinnamon sticks
- 8 whole allspices
- 4 garlic cloves
- 1/2 tbsp salt
- 2-star anise

Directions: Wash the plums thoroughly with water and rinse them. Trim off its roots and stems from the onions then cut them into 1/2-inch pieces. Pack the plums and onions in sterilized jars.
Combine water, wine vinegar in a saucepan and bring the mixture to a boil. Stir in sugar, cinnamon sticks, allspice, garlic cloves, salt and star anise in a saucepan.
Leave the mixture boil until the sugar has dissolved. Remove the mixture from heat. Pour the hot mixture on the jars with plums leaving a 1/4-inch headspace.
Wipe the jar rims, place the lids and rings on the jar. Process the jars in the pressure canner for 40 minutes at 10 pounds pressure.
Wait for the pressure canner to depressurize to zero before removing the jars and cooling them on a wire rack for 12-24 hours.

Nutrition: Calories: 238.7; Fat: 0g; Carbs: 58.7g; Protein: 1.2g

6. Spicy Ginger Red Hot Pears

Preparation Time: 15 minutes **Cooking Time:** 1 hour & 15 minutes
Servings: 5 pints

Ingredients:

- 6 lb. ripe pears
- Ascorbic acid color keeper
- 4-1/2 cups water
- 2 cups sugar
- 6 cinnamon sticks
- 6 tbsp ginger, freshly chopped
- 12 tbsp red cinnamon candies.

Directions: Peel the pears, cut them into halves, core them and cut into small wedges placing them in ascorbic acid.
Prepare the syrup by combining water and sugar in a heavy saucepan. Stir cook until all the sugar has dissolved. Drain the pears into the saucepan with the syrup. Let boil then reduce heat to simmer for 4 minutes while uncovered.
Place a cinnamon stick in each jar, a tablespoon of ginger, and 2 tablespoons of cinnamon candied in each sterilized jar.
Ladle the pears in each jar leaving a 1/2-inch headspace. Wipe the rims, place the lids and place the rings on the jars.
Process the jars in the pressure canner for 70 minutes at 10 pounds pressure. Let the canner cool completely before removing the jars and cooling them on a wire rack.

Nutrition: Calories: 121.8; Fat: 0g; Carbs: 31.9g; Protein: 0g

7. Caramel Apple Butter

Preparation Time: 45 minutes **Cooking Time:** 2 hours & 50 minutes
Servings: 6 pints

Ingredients:

- 4-1/2 lb. tart cooking apples
- 3 cups apple cider
- 1-1/2 cups brown sugar, packed
- 1/2 cup granulated sugar
- 2 tbsp lemon juice
- 1/2 tbsp ground cinnamon

Directions: Cut your apples into quarters, core them and add them to a 10-quart pot. Add apple cider and bring to boil. Reduce heat and simmer while stirring frequently for 35 minutes while covered.
Press the apple mixture through a sieve into a large bowl then discard the seeds and the peels. Measure a 7-1/2 cup of the pulp and return back to the pot.
Put in all other ingredients and bring the mixture to boil. Reduce heat and simmer uncovered for 1-3/4 hours or until the mixture is thick.
Ladle the hot mixture in the sterilized jars leaving a 1/4-inch headspace. Clean the edges and place the lids and the rings on the jars.

Process the jars for 30 minutes at 10 pounds pressure. Let the canner cool before removing the jars and placing them on a cooling rack.

Nutrition: Calories: 27.9; Fat: 0g; Carbs: 6.9g; Protein: 0g

8. Port and Cinnamon Plums

Preparation Time: 25 minutes **Cooking Time: 1 hour & 20 minutes**
Servings: 7 pints

Ingredients:
- 4-1/2 lb. plums
- 1 orange
- 4 cups water
- 2-1/2 cups sugar
- 3/4 cup ruby port
- 1/4 tbsp salt
- 7 3-inch cinnamon sticks

Directions: Quarter the plums and pit them. Cut 3 inches of strips from the orange peel. Squeeze 1/3 cup of juice from your orange
Make the syrup by adding the orange juice in a saucepan then add all other ingredients except the cinnamon sticks. Bring the mixture to boil and stir to dissolve all sugar.
Pack the plums, orange strips and cinnamon sticks in the sterilized jars. Ladle the syrup leaving a 1/2-inch headspace. Wipe the rims; place the lids and the rings on the jars.
Process the jars in the pressure canner for 70 minutes at 10 pounds pressure.
Let the pressure canner depressurize to zero to remove the jars. Transfer the jar to a wire rack and let cool for 24 hours before storing them.

Nutrition: Calories: 124.8; Fat: 0g; Carbs: 29.6g; Protein: 1.1g

9. Apple Jam

Preparation Time: 35 minutes **Cooking Time: 1 hour & 5 minutes**
Servings: 6 pints

Ingredients:
- 4 lb. tart apples
- 2 tbsp lemon juice
- 1-1/4 cups water
- 3 cups sugar, granulated
- 1 cup brown sugar, packed
- 1 tbsp vanilla
- 1 tbsp butter

Directions: Combine apples, lemon juice, and 1/2 cup of water in a shallow saucepan and heat over medium-high heat.
Bring to boil while stirring frequently then reduce heat to simmer for 30 minutes. The apples should be tender.
Press the apples through a sieve until you get 5 cups of the pulp. Discard the seeds and the peels.
Meanwhile, pour granulated sugar on a heavy saucepan and heat it over high heat as you shake the pan.
When the sugar has started to melt, reduce heat, and cook on low heat for 10 minutes.
Remove the melted sugar from heat and add 3/4 cup of water. Return back to the heat and stir cook over medium heat until all sugar has dissolved.
Add the apple pulp and brown sugar to the mixture. Cook over medium-high heat until all caramel and sugar has dissolved.
Let the mixture boil gently for 10 minutes or until it thickens. Take off from heat and stir in vanilla and butter.
Ladle the jam in sterilized jars leaving a 1/4-inch headspace. Wipe jar rims and place the lids and the rings on the jars. Process the jars for 55 minutes at 10 pounds pressure. Let the pressure canners depressurize before removing the jars.
Place the jars on a rack undisturbed for 12-24 hours, then store them in a cool dry place.

Nutrition: Calories: 56.8; Fat: 0g; Carbs: 13.9g; Protein: 0g

10. Green Tea Spiced Peaches

Preparation Time: 15 minutes **Cooking Time: 1 hour & 5 minutes**
Servings: 12 pints

Ingredients:
- 15 pounds ripe peaches
- 4-1/2 cups water
- 1-1/3 cup sugar, granulated
- 1/2 cup brown sugar, packed
- 3-inch piece ginger, fresh peeled and thinly sliced
- 3 inches stick cinnamon
- 10 garlic cloves
- 10 green cardamom pods

- *10 black peppercorns*
- *1 tbsp green tea leaves, loose*

Directions: Bring a large pot of water into boiling. Cook the peaches, in batches, in the boiling water for 30-60 seconds or until the skin starts to peel.

Use a slotted spoon to remove the pitches from the hot water to a large bowl of ice-cold water. Remove the peaches from cold water and peel the skin.

Cut them into half lengthwise and discard the pits. Combine, 4-1/2 cups water, both sugars, ginger, cinnamon, garlic cloves, cardamom pods and peppercorns in a Dutch oven

Stir cook over medium heat until all the sugar has dissolved. Broil to boil then reduce heat and simmer for 20 minutes.

Take off from heat and stir in the green tea leaves. Cover and let rest for 5 minutes. Use a strainer to strain the syrup. Discard the solids.

Pack the peaches in the sterilized jars the ladle the syrup in each jar leaving a 1/2-inch headspace.

Wipe the rims, place the lids and place the rings on the jars. Process the jars for 1 hour at 10 pounds pressure. Wait for the canner to cool to remove the jars. Cool them on a wire rack before storing.

Nutrition: Calories: 68.6; Fat: 0g; Carbs: 16.9g; Protein: 1.2g

CHAPTER 2: VEGETABLES

11. Asparagus Spear
Preparation Time: 15 minutes
Servings: 9 pints
Cooking Time: 30 minutes

Ingredients:
- 16 pounds asparagus spears
- 10 tbsp. salt
- boiling water

Directions: In a large pot, cover the asparagus with boiling water and add salt. Boil for 3 minutes. Fill the sterilized jars loosely with the asparagus and liquid, leaving 1-inch headspace.
Adjust the jar lids and process the jars for 30 minutes in a pressure canner.

Nutrition: Calories: 5.8; Carbs: 0.8g; Fat: 0g; Protein: 0g

12. Tomato Ketchup
Preparation Time: 30 minutes
Canning Time: 10 minutes
Cooking Time: 55 minutes
Servings: 2 pints

Ingredients:
- 2 ½ quarts ripe tomatoes
- 3-inch piece stick cinnamon
- 2 teaspoons mustard seed
- 1 teaspoon whole cloves
- 1 large garlic clove, chopped
- 3 teaspoons celery seed
- ¾ cup onion, diced
- 1 cup apple cider vinegar
- 1 ¼ teaspoons salt
- ½ cup sugar
- 1/8 teaspoon cayenne pepper
- 1 teaspoon paprika

Directions: In a large pot, simmer the tomatoes for 20 minutes and press through a fine sieve to remove seeds. Bring the pulp to a boil and continue boiling until it is reduced by about half.

Place the cinnamon stick, mustard seed, celery seed, onion, garlic, and the whole cloves on a thin, clean white cloth and tie to make a spice bag.
Add the spice bag to the boiling pulp and let it simmer for 30 minutes. Remove the spice bag.
Add the vinegar, sugar, salt, paprika, and cayenne pepper to the tomato mixture. Boil rapidly, stirring constantly, for 5 minutes. Pour into sterile jars, leaving 1-inch headspace.
Adjust the lids and process in the pressure canner for 10 minutes at 10 pounds of pressure for a pressure canner with a weighted gauge.

Nutrition: Calories: 322.9; Fat: 14.8g; Carbs: 22.7g; Fiber: 3.9g; Protein: 25.2g

13. Carrots
Preparation Time: 30 minutes
Canning Time: 30 minutes
Cooking Time: 20 minutes
Servings: 6-pint jars (12 cups)

Ingredients:
- 6–7 pounds carrots
- 2 cups brown sugar
- 2 cups water
- 1 cup orange juice
- 1 tablespoon kosher salt

Directions: Wash, peel, and slice carrots. Slices should be 1–2-inch thick. Mix brown sugar with water and orange juice as well as the carrots in a large saucepot. Bring to a boil. Turn down the flame to medium and cook until. the sugar has dissolved and carrots are almost tender about 10–15 minutes.
Pack the carrots into the jars add salt, and pour the syrup over the carrots.
Process pints and quarts at 10 pounds each for 30 minutes for the weighted gauge of the pressure canner or 11 pounds if the pressure canner has a dial gauge.
Take out the jars, and let them cool completely at room temperature before storing. This can take about a day.

Nutrition: Carbs: 39.1g; Fat: 0.3g; Protein: 2.1g; Calories: 160.2

14. Tomatoes
Preparation Time: 30 minutes
Canning Time: 45 minutes
Cooking Time: 10 minutes
Servings: 7 quarts

Ingredients:
- 21 pounds whole tomatoes, skinned
- 4 tablespoons salt
- ¾ cup lemon juice, optional
- Boiling water

Directions: Place the tomatoes and the salt in a saucepan and cover with the water. Bring to a boil and cook for 5 minutes. Pack sterilized jars with the tomatoes and the hot liquid; leaving a ½-inch headspace, remove any air bubbles, clean the rim and adjust lids.
If omitting the lemon juice, process the jars for 45 minutes in a pressure canner at 10 pounds for a pressure canner with a weighted gauge or 11 pounds if the pressure canner has a gauge.
If using lemon juice, process the jars for 10 minutes in a boiling water bath.

Nutrition: Carbs: 42.1g; Fat: 3.4g; Protein: 13.5g; Calories: 209.8

15. Herbed Tomatoes
Preparation Time: 30 minutes
Servings: 4 pints
Cooking Time: 20 minutes

Ingredients:
- 8 pounds tomatoes, peeled
- Water
- Spiced blend (house seasoning)

Directions: Combine tomatoes and water in a saucepan and let boil.
Add spices and add to canning tomatoes and use pressure cooking method.

Nutrition: Carbs: 46.2g; Fat: 4.1g; Protein: 10.4g; Calories: 237.5

16. Asparagus

Preparation Time: 30 minutes
Canning Time: 30 minutes
Cooking Time: 5 minutes
Servings: 9 pints

Ingredients:
- 16 pounds asparagus spears
- 10 tablespoons salt
- Boiling water

Directions: In a large pot, cover the asparagus with boiling water and add salt. Boil for 3 minutes. Fill sterilized jars loosely with the asparagus and liquid, leaving 1-inch headspace. Adjust the jar lids and process the jars for 30 minutes in a pressure canner at 10 pounds of pressure for a pressure canner with a weighted gauge or 11 pounds if the pressure canner has a dial gauge.

Nutrition: Carbs: 31.1g; Fat: 0.8g; Protein: 17.8g; Calories: 160.9

17. Marinated Mushrooms

Preparation Time: 30 minutes
Canning Time: 20 minutes
Cooking Time: 15 minutes
Servings: 9 pints

Ingredients:
- ¼ cup pimiento, diced
- ½ cup lemon juice, bottled
- 1 tablespoon basil leaves, dried
- 2 ½ cups white vinegar, 5%
- ½ cup onions, chopped finely
- 7 pounds mushrooms, small, whole
- 2 cups oil, olive/salad
- 1 tablespoon oregano leaves
- 1 tablespoon pickling/canning salt
- 25 pieces black peppercorns
- Water
- Garlic clove

Directions: Make sure your mushrooms are very fresh, still unopened, and have caps with a diameter of less than 1 ¼ inches.
Wash the mushrooms before cutting the stems, but leave a quarter of an inch still attached to their caps. Place in a saucepan and cover with water and lemon juice. Heat until boiling, and then simmer for 5 minutes before draining.
Add the vinegar, salt, basil, oregano, and olive oil to a saucepan. Stir to combine as you also add the pimiento and onions. Heat the mixture until boiling.
Meanwhile, fill each of your clean and hot Mason jars (half-pint) with garlic clove (1/4 portion) and peppercorns (2 to 3 pieces)
Add the cooked mushrooms as well as the hot liquid mixture, making sure to leave half an inch of headspace. Take out any air bubbles before adjusting the lids. Put in the pressure canner and process for 20 minutes.

Nutrition: Carbs: 2.7g; Fat: 48.1g; Protein: 0.6g; Calories: 450.9

18. Herbed Peas

Preparation Time: 10 minutes
Serving Size: 4 pints
Cooking Time: 20 minutes

Ingredients:
- 3 pounds peas
- Chervil, as needed
- Thyme, as needed
- Water

Directions: You will use the pressure canner with this one.
Wash and dry peas and shell and wash again.
Boil the peas, pack hot peas in jars, add seasoning, and use a pressure cooker.

Nutrition: Calories: 279.8; Fat: 7.6g; Fiber: 1.8g; Carbs: 6.9g; Protein: 8.2g

19. Cabbage with Beans

Preparation Time: 15 minutes
Servings: 6
Cooking Time: 2 hours & 20 minutes

Ingredients:
- 3 tbsps. extra-virgin olive oil
- 1 diced onion
- 6 minced garlic cloves
- 1 grated ginger
- 2 tbsps. yellow curry powder
- 2 tsp. paprika
- 2 tsp. cayenne pepper
- 1 tsp. salt
- 1 sliced cabbage head
- 3 diced tomatoes
- 1 chopped yellow bell pepper
- 1 chopped red bell pepper
- 1 shredded carrot
- 2 cups chicken or vegetable stock
- 1 can great northern beans

Directions: Combine the oil, onion, garlic, ginger, curry powder, paprika, cayenne, and salt in a sizable pot. Cook on medium heat for 8 minutes until the onion softens. Add the cabbage and mix well to coat. Cook for an additional 5 minutes to slightly soften the cabbage.

Add the tomatoes, bell peppers, and carrot. Cook for an additional 10 minutes to blend the flavors, often stirring to distribute the flavors.

Add the chicken stock and beans, and mix well. Boil as you stir for 10 minutes.

Arrange the hot jars on a cutting board. Using a funnel, ladle the hot cabbage and beans into the jars, leaving 1-inch headspace.

Eliminate any air bubbles and add additional mixture or cabbage liquid if necessary to maintain the 1-inch headspace.

Rinse the jar rims with a warm towel dipped in distilled white vinegar, then seal the lids. Fill 3 quarts of water and add 2 tablespoons of distilled white vinegar to the pressure canner.

Arrange the jars in the pressure canner, lock the pressure canner lid, and bring to a boil over high heat.

Let the canner vent for 10 minutes. Close the vent and continue heating to reach 11 PSI (dial gauge) and 10 PSI (weighted gauge). Can the quarts for 90 minutes and pints for 75 minutes.

Nutrition: Calories: 168.7; Carbs: 14.9g; Fat: 7.9g; Protein: 10.3g

20. Asparagus Spears

Preparation Time: 35 minutes **Cooking Time: 5 minutes**
Canning Time: 30 minutes **Servings: 12-pint jars**

Ingredients:
- 16 pounds asparagus spears
- 10 tablespoons salt
- Boiling water

Directions: In a large pot, cover the asparagus with boiling water and add salt. Boil for 3 minutes. Fill sterilized jars loosely with the asparagus and liquid, leaving 1-inch headspace.

Adjust the jar lids and process the jars for 30 minutes in a pressure canner at 10 pounds of pressure for a pressure canner with a weighted gauge or 11 pounds if the pressure canner has a dial gauge.

Nutrition: Calories: 339.9; Fat: 22.7g; Fiber: 1.8g; Carbs: 7.8g; Protein: 28.3g

21. Corn Kernel

Preparation Time: 35 minutes **Cooking Time: 5 minutes**
Canning Time: 55 minutes **Servings: 9-pint jars**

Ingredients:
- 20 pounds corn, cut from the cob
- 9 teaspoons salt
- 10 cups water

Directions: In a large pan, add water, salt, and corn and bring to a boil. Let it boil for 5 minutes.

Fill sterilized jars with the corn and the liquid, leaving 1-inch headspace.

Adjust the jar lids and process the jars in a pressure canner for 55 minutes at 10 pounds of pressure for a pressure canner with a weighted gauge or 11 pounds if the pressure canner has a gauge.

Nutrition: Calories: 339.8; Fat: 22.7g; Fiber: 1.9g; Carbs: 7.5g; Protein: 28.3g

22. White Potatoes

Preparation Time: 35 minutes **Cooking Time: 15 minutes**
Canning Time: 35 minutes **Servings: 9-pint jars**

Ingredients:
- 13 pounds potatoes
- 4 tablespoons salt
- Boiling water

Directions: Wash and peel the potatoes and place them in an ascorbic acid solution, made up of 1 gallon of water with 1 cup of lemon juice to prevent them from darkening. If you do not want whole potatoes, cut them into ½-inch cubes. Drain and cook for 2 minutes in boiling salted water, and drain again.

For whole potatoes, boil in salted water for 10 minutes and drain.

Fill sterilized jars with the potatoes. Cover the potatoes with fresh boiling water, leaving 1-inch headspace.

Process in a pressure canner for 35 minutes at 10 pounds of pressure for a pressure canner with a weighted gauge or 11 pounds if the pressure canner has a gauge.

Nutrition: Calories: 269.9; Fat: 17.9g; Fiber: 0.8g; Carbs: 2.8g; Protein: 22.3g

23. Tomatoes—Whole

Preparation Time: 35 minutes
Canning Time: 45 minutes
Cooking Time: 5 minutes
Servings: 7-pint jars

Ingredients:
- 21 pounds whole tomatoes, skinned
- 4 tablespoons salt
- ¾ cup lemon juice, optional
- Boiling water

Directions: Place the tomatoes and the salt in a saucepan and cover with water. Bring to a boil and cook for 5 minutes.

Pack sterilized jars with the tomatoes and the hot liquid, leaving a ½-inch headspace. Remove any air bubbles, clean the rim, and adjust the lids.

If omitting the lemon juice, process the jars for 45 minutes in a pressure canner at 10 pounds for a pressure canner with a weighted gauge (or 11 pounds if the pressure canner has a dial gauge).

If using lemon juice, process the jars for 10 minutes in a boiling water bath.

Nutrition: Calories: 269.8; Fat: 17.9g; Fiber: 0.9g; Carbs: 2.7g; Protein: 22.3g

24. Canned Asparagus

Preparation Time: 35 minutes
Canning Time: 40 minutes
Cooking Time: 10 minutes
Servings: 9-quart jars

Ingredients:
- 10 pounds asparagus
- Canning salt
- Boiling water

Directions: First, bring the water to boil using a pot over high heat.

Trim the asparagus so that they fit in the jars. Pack them in the jars, add 1/2 tablespoon of salt and the boiling water leaving 1-inch headspace.

Wipe the jar rims, place the lids, place the rings, and use your hands to tighten.

After which, put the jars in the pressure canner and process at 10 pounds for a minimum of 30 minutes for pints and at least 40 minutes for quarts. Allow the pressure canner to depressurize before removing the jars.

Nutrition: Calorie: 51.9; Fat: 0.9g; Carbs: 54.7g; Protein: 2.1g

25. Canned Plain Beets

Preparation Time: 35 minutes
Canning Time: 30 minutes
Cooking Time: 25 minutes
Servings: 3-quart jars

Ingredients:
- 1 pound beets
- Water
- Pickling salt

Directions: Trim the tops of the beets leaving an inch-long top. Also, leave the roots on the beets.

Wash the beets thoroughly with clean water then put them in a pot.

Cover the beets with water and bring to boil for 15–25 minutes or until the skin can come out easily.

Remove the beets from hot water and let them cool a little bit so that you can hold them. They should be at least warm when being put in the jar.

Trim the remaining stem and roots then peel the beets.

Slice the beets into large slices leaving the small ones whole. Put the beets in jars and leave a 1-inch headspace.

Add a half tablespoon of salt in each jar then add boiling water in each jar.

Remove any bubbles in the jar then wipe the rims with a clean piece of cloth.

Put on the lids and the rings. Process the jars at 10 pounds for 30 minutes.

Let the pressure canner depressurize to zero before removing the jars.

Nutrition: Calories: 51.8; Fat: 0.9g; Carbs: 54.7g; Protein: 2.1g

26. Hot Peppers

Preparation Time: 35 minutes
Canning Time: 35 minutes
Cooking Time: 10 minutes
Servings: 2-pint jars

Ingredients:
- 2 pounds hot peppers
- Salt
- Boiling water

Directions: Wear rubber gloves on your hands to avoid a burning sensation.
Sort the peppers and select the fresh and firm ones for maximum results.
Wash the hot peppers and place them on a lined baking sheet in a single layer.
Broil in the broiler for 5–10 minutes making sure you flip over once.
Transfer the hot pepper to a zip lock bag and seal tightly. Let rest for 10 minutes then remove them from the bag.
Rub off as much pepper skin as possible.
Trim the tops off, scrape out the seeds, then cut the peppers into two or into sizes that will fit in the jar.
Pack the peppers in the jars then add a half tablespoon of salt to each jar. Add boiling water to each jar leaving 1-inch headspace.
Wipe the rims, close the lids and place the rings in place. Process the jars for 35 minutes at 10 pounds pressure.
Wait for the scanner to depressurize before removing the jars out.
Nutrition: Calories: 99.8; Fat: 6.9g; Fiber: 1.7g; Carbs: 7.9g; Protein: 6.2g

27. Canned Kale

Preparation Time: 15 minutes **Cooking Time: 1 hour & 20 minutes**
Servings: 5 pints

Ingredients:
- *10 lb. kale*
- *Water*
- *Salt*

Directions: Chop the kale into bite-size pieces, then remove all the kale's hard stems and yellow parts. Add the cleaned kale to the stockpot. Cover the kale with water.
Bring the water to a boil until the kale has wilted nicely. Use a slotted spoon to fill the jars with kale, then add ½ tablespoon salt in each jar. Add the cooking liquid and leave a 1-inch headspace.
Remove any air bubbles and add more cooking liquid if necessary. Clean the rims and place the lids and rings on the jars. Process the jars at 10-11 pounds of pressure for 70 minutes.
Switch off the heat and let the canner cool before using a jar lifer to remove the jars. Let rest for 24 hours undisturbed before storing them in a cool, dry place.
Nutrition: Calories: 34.9; Carbs: 3.8g; Fat: 0.7g; Protein: 3.1g

28. Sweet Peppers

Preparation Time: 35 minutes **Cooking Time: 5 minutes**
Canning Time: 35 minutes **Servings: 2-pint jars**

Ingredients:
- *2 pounds sweet bell peppers*
- *Salt*
- *Water*

Directions: Thoroughly wash the sweet bell peppers then cut them into quarters.
Place the peppers in a pot covered with water and bring to boil for 3 minutes.
Transfer the peppers to the pint jars then add a quarter tablespoon of salt in each jar.
Ladle the cooking liquid in each jar leaving 1-inch headspace. Make sure to wipe the rims and place the lids and rings. After which, place the jars in the pressure canner and process for 35 minutes at 10 pounds pressure.
Let the pressure canner depressurize before removing the jars.
Nutrition: Calories: 199.8; Fat: 7.9g; Fiber: 1.9g; Carbs: 7.7g; Protein: 6.2g

29. Canned Turnips

Preparation Time: 35 minutes **Cooking Time: 10 minutes**
Canning Time: 30 minutes **Servings: 12-pint jars**

Ingredients:
- *10 pounds turnips*
- *Water*

Directions: Peel the turnips then dice them into small pieces.
Add the turnips to a stockpot and add cold water until just covered. Drain the water to get rid of dirt and debris.
Cover with water once more and bring them to boil over medium-high heat. Diminish the heat and let simmer for 5 minutes.
Utilize a slotted spoon to transfer the hot turnips in sterilized jars. Fill the jar with the cooking liquid leaving 1-inch headspace. Add a half tablespoon of pickling salt.

Remove any air bubbles and add the cooking liquid if necessary. Wipe the pint jars and place the lids and rings. Load the jars into the pressure canner and process at 10 pounds for 30 minutes.
Allow the canner to depressurize to zero before removing the jars.

Nutrition: Calories: 197.9; Fat: 11.9g; Fiber: 1.8g; Carbs: 19.9g; Protein: 5.1g

30. Caramelized Onions

Preparation Time: 35 minutes
Canning Time: 70 minutes

Cooking Time: 11 hours
Servings: 6-pint jars

Ingredients:
- 6 pounds onions
- 2 butter sticks
- Water

Directions: Peel the onions and also slice them into ¼-inch slices.
Melt 1 stick of butter in the stockpot over high heat then add the diced onions.
Slice another stick of butter over the onions. Cook on high for an hour until the butter has melted and the onions were sweating a little bit.
Reduce the heat then let cook for 10 hours or overnight while stirring occasionally. The onions should be golden brown and well caramelized.
Ladle the onions in the sterilized hot jars then remove any air bubbles. Also, wipe the jar rims with a damp clean cloth. Place the lid and rings on the jars and process them at 10 pounds pressure for 70 minutes.
Remove the pressure canner from heat and let its pressure reduce to zero before removing the jars.

Nutrition: Calories: 197.9; Fat: 11.7g; Fiber: 1.8g; Carbs: 19.9g; Protein: 5.2g

31. Fiddleheads

Preparation Time: 35 minutes
Canning Time: 10 minutes

Cooking Time: 20 minutes
Servings: 1-pint jar

Ingredients:
- 2 cups fiddleheads
- ½ cup water
- ½ cup white vinegar
- 1 tablespoon salt
- ½ tablespoon peppercorns
- ½ tablespoon fennel
- ½ tablespoon coriander
- 1 sprig thyme
- 3 garlic cloves

Directions: Trim off the cut ends then boil the fiddleheads for 10 minutes in salted water.
Strain the fiddleheads and rinse them with clean water. Pack the fiddleheads in the jars and leave a 1-inch headspace.
Add the spices directly to each jar on top of the fiddleheads.
Boil water, vinegar, and salt in a saucepan and pour over the fiddleheads.
Wipe the rims, then place the lids and the rings on the jars. After which, place the jars in the pressure canner and process at 10 pounds pressure for 10 minutes.

Nutrition: Calories: 339.7; Fat: 22.9g; Fiber: 1.8g; Carbs: 7.7g; Protein: 28.1g

32. Glazed Carrots

Preparation Time: 15 minutes
Servings: 16 pints

Cooking Time: 30 minutes

Ingredients:
- 8 cups of sugar, brown
- About 10 pounds of carrots
- 4 cups of orange juice
- 8 cups of water, filtered

Directions: Wash carrots and drain them. Combine orange juice, brown sugar, and water in a large-sized saucepan. Heat on medium heat and stir till sugar dissolves. Keep mixture hot.
Place the raw carrots in the sterilized, hot jars. Leave an inch of headspace. Fill the jars with the hot syrup, still leaving an inch of headspace.
Tap the jars to remove any air bubbles. Wipe jar rims and screw on the lids. Process jars in a pressure canner for 1/2 hour under 10 pounds of pressure. Store in a cool, dry area.

Nutrition: Calories: 76.9; Carbs: 1.8g; Fat: 1.9g; Protein: 0g

33. Canned Carrots

Preparation Time: 15 minutes **Cooking Time: 25 minutes**
Servings: 7

Ingredients:
- 2 ½ lb. carrots
- 1 tbsp. salt
- 1 cup water

Directions: Wash the carrots and trim them. Peel the carrots and wash them again, if you desire. Slice the carrots into pieces according to your preferences.
Pack the carrots in the jars, leaving 1-inch headspace. Add a ½ tablespoon of salt to each jar, then add boiling water to each jar.
Rinse the jar rims with a clean, damp towel, and place the lids on the jars. Arrange the jars in the pressure canner and process them for 25 minutes at 10 pounds of pressure.
Let the canner rest and depressurize before removing the jars.

Nutrition: Calories: 51.8; Carbs: 11.9g; Fat: 0g; Protein: 1.2g

34. Canned Potatoes

Preparation Time: 1- minutes **Cooking Time: 40 minutes**
Servings: 7

Ingredients:
- 6 lb. cubed white potatoes
- Canning salt

Directions: Wash the jars thoroughly, then place them in a cold oven. Heat it to 250°F. Boil water in a pot. Also, add 4 inches of water in the pressure canner and place it over medium heat.
Add some salt in each jar, then fill with potatoes, leaving 1-inch headspace. Pour the boiling water into each jar, then use a canning knife to remove the air bubbles from the jars.
Rinse the jar rims and place the lids and rings on the jars. Arrange the jars in the pressure canner and secure the lid according to the manufacturer's instructions.
Process the jars at 10 pounds for 40 minutes and 35 minutes for pint jars. Turn off the heat and let the canner depressurize before removing the jars.
Place the jars on a towel, undisturbed, for 24 hours. Store in a cool, dry place.

Nutrition: Calories: 69.9; Carbs: 14.7g; Fat: 0g; Protein: 1.2g

35. Canned Sweet Potatoes

Preparation Time: 15 minutes **Cooking Time: 1 hour & 40 minutes**
Servings: 10 quarts

Ingredients:
- 10 lb. sweet potatoes
- water
- 1½ cups sugar

Directions: Add the whole sweet potatoes to a stockpot, then add water until they are covered. Bring to a boil for 15 minutes.
Drain the sweet potatoes and set them aside to cool so they can be easily peeled. Cut them into large chunks, then pack them in the clean jars leaving a half-inch headspace.
Boil 3 cups of water and add 1 ½ cups of brown sugar until the sugar has dissolved.
Add boiled water to some of the jars and simple brown sugar syrup to others but maintain the headspace. Remove the bubbles and add more hot water if necessary.
Wipe the jar rims, then place the lids and rings on. Transfer the jars into the canner and process at 10 pounds for 90 minutes for quart jars and 65 minutes for pint jars.
Let the pressure drop so that you can remove the jars from the canner.

Nutrition: Calories: 149.9; Carbs: 35.8g; Fat: 0g; Protein: 1.2g

36. Pressure Canned Tomatoes

Preparation Time: 15 minutes
Servings: 6
Cooking Time: 1 hour & 30 minutes

Ingredients:
- 9 lb. ripe peeled and halved tomatoes
- 1 tbsp. lemon juice
- 1 tbsp. salt

Directions: Pack the tomatoes in the sterilized jars while pressing them down so that the space between the tomato pieces is filled with their juices.
Leave a ½-inch headspace. Add a tablespoon of lemon juice and ½ tablespoons of salt to each jar. Rinse the rims and place the lids and the rings on the jars.
Transfer to the pressure cooker for 1 hour and 30 minutes at 10 pounds of pressure. Wait for the pressure canner to depressurize to remove the jars. Place the jars on a cooling rack, then store them in a cool, dry place.

Nutrition: Calories: 59.8; Carbs: 14.9g; Fat: 0g; Protein: 4.2g

37. Shelled Lima Beans

Preparation Time: 15 minutes
Servings: 9 pints
Cooking Time: 50 minutes

Ingredients:
- 18 pounds lima beans, shelled
- 10 tablespoons salt
- Boiling water

Directions: In a large pot, cover the beans with boiling water and add salt. Boil the beans for 10 minutes. Fill the sterilized jars loosely with beans and liquid, leaving 1-inch headspace.
Adjust the jar lids and process the jars for 40 minutes in a pressure canner at 10 pounds of pressure for a pressure canner with a weighted gauge (or 11 pounds if the pressure canner has a dial gauge).

Nutrition: Calories: 99.8; Carbs: 18.7g; Fat: 0g; Protein: 7.2g

38. Canned Broccoli

Preparation Time: 15 minutes
Servings: 4 half pints
Cooking Time: 33 minutes

Ingredients:
- Fresh broccoli
- Canning salt
- Water

Directions: Wash broccoli well. Cut the heads into two-inch long pieces, discard or save the stem for other things if desired.
Put broccoli in boiling and boil for 3 minutes. Then, pack into jars, cover with boiling water, leaving 1 inch headspace. Add 1 tsp canning salt to each jar.
Process jar at 10 lbs. pressure for 30 minutes. Let cool for 12 hours and remove.

Nutrition: Calories: 7.9; Fat 0.1g; Carbs: 1.3g; Protein: 0.6g

39. Blue Ribbon Green Beans

Preparation Time: 15 minutes
Servings: 4 pints
Cooking Time: 20 minutes

Ingredients:
- ½ to ¾ lbs. green bush beans per pint
- ½ tsp salt per pint, optional

Directions: Wash and snap the beans to fit jars. Raw pack beans into jars. In a pan, broil water to a boil, and add salt if desired. Stir to dissolve.
Pour boiling into jars over the beans, leaving 1 inch headspace. Process jars for 20 minutes at 10 pounds of pressure. Let cool for 12 hours and remove.

Nutrition: Calories: 94.8; Fat: 2.3g; Carbs: 10.5g; Protein: 8.4g

40. Canned Parsnips

Preparation Time: 15 minutes **Cooking Time: 30 minutes**
Servings: 4 pints

Ingredients:
- ½ lbs. parsnips per pint jar
- Salt, optional
- Water

Directions: Wash parsnips thoroughly, then cut them into chunks about two inches in size. Then blanch for four minutes in boiling water, then dip in an ice bath.
Pack parsnips into jars, then pour in boiling water into jars, leaving 1 inch headspace. Add salt if preferred.
Process jars for 30 minutes at 10 pounds pressure or 11 pounds with a dial gauge. Once done, let cool for 12-24 hours before removing

Nutrition: Calories: 74.8; Protein: 4.2g; Carbs: 23.9g; Fat: 0.4g

41. Canned Succotash

Preparation Time: 15 minutes **Cooking Time: 60 minutes**
Servings: 5 pints

Ingredients:
- 2 ½ tsp coarse salt, divided
- ¾ pound fresh lima beans
- 10 ears corn, shucked

Directions: Bring a large pot of water to a boil, then add corn, cook until tender for 4 minutes. When cool enough, cut off kernels and combine with beans.
Put ½ tsp salt in each jar, and 1 ½ cups hot succotash, leaving 1 inch headspace.
Process jars at 11 pounds pressure for an hour. Then, let cool naturally over 6 hours before removal.

Nutrition: Calories: 179.9; Carbs: 37.8g; Protein: 8.1g; Fats: 0g

CHAPTER 3: MEAT, SEAFOOD AND POULTRY

42. Hearty Chili
Preparation Time: 15 minutes
Canning Time: 90 minutes
Cooking Time: 55 minutes
Servings: 6 pints

Ingredients:
- 4 pounds boneless beef chuck, cut into ½ inch cubes
- ¼ cup vegetable oil
- 3 cups onion, diced
- 2 garlic cloves, minced
- 5 tablespoons chili powder
- 2 teaspoons cumin seed
- 2 teaspoons salt
- 1 teaspoons oregano
- ½ teaspoon pepper
- ½ teaspoon coriander
- ½ teaspoon crushed red pepper
- 6 cups diced canned tomatoes and their juices

Directions: In a pot, add the oil and lightly brown the meat.
Mix the garlic and onions and cook for 5 minutes. Add the remaining spices and cook for 5 minutes and then, put the tomatoes and broil to a boil. Lower the flame and let this simmer for 45 minutes, stirring occasionally. Pour the chili into sterile jars, leaving 1-inch headspace. Wipe the jar rims clean and adjust the tops.
Process the filled jars in a pressure canner for 90 minutes at 10 pounds of pressure for a pressure canner with a weighted gauge (or 11 pounds if the pressure canner has a dial gauge).

Nutrition: Calories: 206.8; Fat: 7.9g; Fiber: 1.9g; Carbs: 7.6g; Protein: 6.2g

43. Canned Tuna

Preparation Time: 20 minutes **Canning Time:** 100 minutes
Servings: 6 pints

Ingredients:
- *5 pounds tuna*
- *Salt*

Directions: Use a sharp kitchen knife to peel off the skin then scrape the surface to remove the blood vessels. Cut the fish lengthwise, then into pieces that fit in a pint jar. Add salt to each jar.
If you have precooked the tuna, add the fish, some vegetable oil, and a tablespoon of salt per pint jar.
Clean the edges and place the lids and the rings on the jars. Process the jars at 10 pounds pressure for 100 minutes. Wait for the pressure canner to depressurize to zero before removing the jars.
Put the jars on a cooling rack for 24 hours then store in a cool dry place.

Nutrition: Calories: 190.8; Fat: 1.3g; Carbs: 0g; Protein: 42.3g

44. Minced Clams

Preparation Time: 20 minutes **Cooking Time:** 10 minutes
Canning Time: 60 minutes **Servings:** 5 pints

Ingredients:
- *5 pounds Clam*
- *3 tablespoons salt*
- *2 tablespoons lemon juice*

Directions: Keep the clams cold in ice until you are ready to pressure-can them.
Scrub the shells then stream them over water for 5 minutes. Open the clams and remove the meat. Save the juices.
Add a gallon of water in a mixing bowl then add at most 3 tablespoons of salt. Wash the clam meat in the salted water. Add water in a shallow saucepan then add lemon juice. Bring the water to a boil. Add the clam meat and boil for 2 minutes. Heat the reserved clam juices until boiling.
Drain the meat and add it to the grinder or a food processor.
Pack 3/4 cup of minced clams in a half-pint leaving a headspace of 1 inch. Add the clam juices, maintaining the headspace.
Remove any air bubbles and add more clam juice if necessary. In case you run out of clam juice, add boiling water.
Clean the edges and place the lids and the rings on the half-pint jars. Process the jars at 10 pounds pressure for 60 minutes. Wait for the pressure canner to depressurize to zero before removing the jars.
Place the jars on a cooling rack undisturbed then store in a cool dry place.

Nutrition: Calories: 147.9; Fat: 1.8g; Carbs: 4.8g; Protein: 25.7g

45. Canned Shrimp

Preparation Time: 20 minutes **Cooking Time:** 10 minutes
Canning Time: 45 minutes **Servings:** 10 pints

Ingredients:
- *10 pounds Shrimp*
- *¼ cup salt*
- *1 cup vinegar*
- *1-gallon water*

Directions: Remove the heads immediately after you catch shrimp then chill until ready to preserve them.
Wash the shrimps and drain them well.
Add a gallon of water to a pot then add salt and vinegar. Bring to a boil then cook shrimp for 10 minutes.
Use a slotted spoon to scoop the shrimp from the cooking liquid then rinse it in cold water and drain. Peel the shrimp while packing it in the sterilized jars.
Add a gallon of water with 3 tablespoons of salt and bring it to a boil. Add the brine to the jars and remove the air bubbles. Add more brine if necessary. Wipe the jar rims with a cloth damped in vinegar. Place the lids and the rings. Process the jars at 10 pounds pressure for 45 minutes
Wait for the pressure canner to depressurize to zero before removing the jars.
Place the jars on a cooling rack undisturbed then store in a cool dry place

Nutrition: Calories: 99.8; Fat: 1.9g; Carbs: 0.8g; Protein: 15.2g

46. Pot Roast in a Jar

Preparation Time: 20 minutes **Cooking Time: 25 minutes**
Canning Time: 25 minutes **Servings: 6**

Ingredients:
- 2 pounds stewing beef, cut into chunks
- 1 cup chopped onions
- 2 teaspoons dried thyme
- 2 garlic cloves, minced
- 2 bay leaves
- 1 cup beef broth
- 1 cup dry red wine
- 2 teaspoons salt
- 1 teaspoon ground black pepper
- 1 cup chopped carrots
- 1 cup diced potatoes
- ½ cup chopped celery

Directions: Sterilize the jars in a pressure canner as indicated in the general guidelines of this book. Allow the jars to cool.
Place the beef in a pot and add in the onions, thyme, garlic, bay leaves, broth, and wine. Season with salt and black pepper. Cover and turn on the heat. Bring to a boil for 10 minutes and allow it to simmer for 10 minutes. Add in the vegetables and simmer for another 5 minutes. Turn off the heat.
Transfer the mixture to sterilized jars. Remove the air bubbles and close the lid.
Place the jars in the pressure canner. Place it in a pressure canner and process for 25 minutes.

Nutrition: Calories: 233.8; Protein: 34.4g; Sugar: 1.9g ; Fat: 5.9g; Carbs: 9.1g

47. Canned Ground Beef

Preparation Time: 15 minutes **Cooking Time: 10 minutes**
Canning Time: 25 minutes **Servings: 5**

Ingredients:
- 2 pounds ground beef
- 3 cups water
- Pickling salt

Directions: Sterilize the jars in a pressure canner as indicated in the general guidelines of this book. Allow the jars to cool. Place the beef in a skillet and sauté the meat for 10 minutes until browned.
Pack the meat loosely in the sterilized jars. Set aside.
In a pan, bring water to a boil and add ½ teaspoon canning salt per pint of water. Stir to dissolve the salt. Pour the canning liquid over the beef and leave a 1-inch headspace. Remove the air bubbles and close the lid.
Place the jars in the pressure canner. Place in a pressure canner and process for 25 minutes.

Nutrition: Calories: 391.8; Protein: 48.5g; Sugar: 0g; Fat: 20.1g; Carbs: 0.5g

48. Chipotle Beef

Preparation Time: 15 minutes **Cooking Time: 25 minutes**
Canning Time: 25 minutes **Servings: 6**

Ingredients:
- 2 pounds beef brisket, cut into chunks
- 2 teaspoons salt
- 8 garlic cloves, minced
- 2 cups onion, chopped
- 2 teaspoons oregano
- ½ cup coriander
- 2 chipotle chilies, chopped
- 4 cups beef broth

Directions: Sterilize the jars in a pressure canner as indicated in the general guidelines of this book. Allow the jars to cool.
Place the beef in a pot and season with salt. Turn on the heat and sear all sides for 3 minutes. Stir in the garlic and onion. Cook for another minute. Add in the rest of the ingredients.
Close the lid and allow the meat to simmer for 20 minutes on medium heat. Turn off the heat and allow the mixture to slightly cool. Transfer the mixture to the jars. Remove the air bubbles and close the lid.
Place the jars in the pressure canner. Place in a pressure canner and process for 25 minutes.

Nutrition: Calories: 321.8; Protein: 23.2g; Sugar: 1.5g; Fat: 21.7g; Carbs: 5.2g

49. Canned Goulash

Preparation Time: 15 minutes
Canning Time: 25 minutes
Cooking Time: 20 minutes
Servings: 5

Ingredients:

- 4 pounds stewing beef, cut into chunks
- 1 cup Peppercorns
- 3 bay leaves
- 2 teaspoons caraway seeds
- 1/3 cup vegetable oil
- 3 onions, chopped
- 1 tablespoon salt
- 6 celery stalks, chopped
- 4 carrots, peeled and chopped
- 2 teaspoons mustard powder
- 1 ½ cups water
- 1/3 cup vinegar

Directions: Sterilize the jars in a pressure canner as indicated in the general guidelines of this book. Allow the jars to cool.
Put the meat in a bowl and add in the peppercorns, bay leaves, and caraway seeds. Massage the beef and allow it to marinate for an hour in the fridge.
Heat oil in a saucepan over medium flame. Sauté the onions for one minute until fragrant and stir in the seasoned beef. Season with salt to taste before adding the rest of the ingredients.
Close the lid and bring to a boil for 5 minutes. Simmer for 15 minutes. Turn off the heat and allow it to cool slightly. Transfer the mixture to the jars. Remove the air bubbles and close the lid.
Place the jars in the pressure canner. Place in a pressure canner and process for 25 minutes.

Nutrition: Calories: 626.8; Protein: 81.2g; Sugar: 4.1g; Fat: 29.1g; Carbs: 11.3g

50. Canned Chicken and Gravy

Preparation Time: 10 minutes
Canning Time: 25 minutes
Cooking Time: 10 minutes
Servings: 5

Ingredients:

- 1 cup chopped onion
- 1 cup chopped celery
- 1 cup diced potatoes
- 2 pounds boneless chicken breasts
- 2 teaspoons salt
- 2 teaspoons poultry seasoning
- 4 tablespoons white wine
- Enough chicken stock to fill the jars

Directions: Sterilize the jars in a pressure canner as indicated in the general guidelines of this book. Allow the jars to cool.
Place all ingredients in a saucepan and allow them to simmer for 10 minutes over medium-high heat.
Put the chicken and vegetables into the jars. Pour over enough broth to cover the chicken. Leave a ½-inch headspace. Remove the air bubbles and close the lid.
Place the jars in the pressure canner. Place in a pressure canner and process for 25 minutes.

Nutrition: Calories: 561.8; Protein: 77.9g; Sugar: 0g; Fat: 22.1g; Carbs: 6.8g

51. Canned Meatballs

Preparation Time: 10 minutes
Canning Time: 25 minutes
Cooking Time: 5 minutes
Servings: 5

Ingredients:

- 2 pounds ground meat
- 1 tps. Herbs of your choice
- 2 teaspoons salt
- Tomato juice to cover the meatballs

Directions: Sterilize the jars in a pressure canner as indicated in the general guidelines of this book. Allow the jars to cool. Put meat in a bowl and stir in the herbs and salt. Mix until well combined.
Boil enough water in a saucepan. Make balls out of the ground meat mixture and gently drop them into the boiling water. Allow it to cook for 5 minutes, then strain the meatballs.
Gently pack the meatballs inside the sterilized jars. Pour in enough tomato juice over the meatballs. Leave an inch of headspace. Remove the air bubbles and close the lid.
Place the jars in the pressure canner. Place it in a pressure canner and process for 25 minutes.

Nutrition: Calories: 271.8; Protein: 35.9g; Sugar: 0g ; Fat: 13.8g; Carbs: 0.6g

52. Canned Pork

Preparation Time: 10 minutes **Cooking Time: 15 minutes**
Canning Time: 25 minutes **Servings: 5**

Ingredients:
- 2 pounds pork chops, boneless
- Canning salt
- Water

Directions: Sterilize the jars in a pressure canner as indicated in the general guidelines of this book. Allow the jars to cool. Place the pork chops in boiling water and allow it to simmer for 15 minutes. Strain the cooked pork and pack them in the sterilized jars.
In a pan, bring water to a boil and add ½ teaspoon of canning salt per pint of water. Stir to dissolve the salt.
Pour pickling solution into the jar to cover the pork. Leave an inch of headspace.
Remove the air bubbles and close the lid.
Place the jars in the pressure canner. Place it in a pressure canner and process for 25 minutes.

Nutrition: Calories: 378.9; Protein: 46.8g; Carbs: 0g; Fat: 19.8g; Sugar: 0 g

53. Canned Turkey

Preparation Time: 10 minutes **Cooking Time: 15 minutes**
Canning Time: 25 minutes **Servings: 5**

Ingredients:
- 2 pounds turkey breasts, sliced into bite-sized pieces
- Canning salt
- Water

Directions: Sterilize the jars in a pressure canner as indicated in the general guidelines of this book. Allow the jars to cool.
Place the turkey breasts in boiling water and allow them to simmer for 10 minutes. Strain the cooked turkey and pack them in the sterilized jars.
In a pan, bring water to a boil and add ½ teaspoon of canning salt per pint of water. Stir to dissolve the salt.
Pour pickling solution into the jar to cover the turkey. Leave an inch of headspace.
Remove the air bubbles and close the lid.
Place the jars in the pressure canner. Place in a pressure canner and process for 25 minutes.

Nutrition: Calories: 284.8; Protein: 39.8g; Sugar: 0g; Fat: 12.5g; Carbs: 0g

54. Ground Beef and Cabbage Soup

Preparation Time: 15 minutes **Cooking Time: 35 minutes**
Canning Time: 1 ¼ hour **Servings: 20**

Ingredients:
- 2 Pounds ground beef
- 1 large onion, chopped
- 2 garlic cloves, minced
- 6 cups cabbage, shredded
- 1 cup celery, chopped
- 1 cup bell pepper, seeded and chopped
- 2 (16-ounce) cans of kidney beans
- 8 cups canned tomatoes with juice
- 8 cups beef broth
- 2 tablespoons garlic powder
- 2 tablespoons dried basil
- 1 tablespoon dried parsley
- 1 tablespoon dried oregano

Directions: Heat a pot over medium-high heat and cook the beef for about 8–10 minutes, crumbling it with the spoon. With a slotted spoon, transfer the cooked beef into a bowl.
Drain the grease, reserving 2 tablespoons inside. In the pan, put the garlic and onion and sauté for about 4–5 minutes. Stir in the cooked beef and the remaining ingredients and cook until boiling.
Now set the heat to low and cook, covered, for about 20 minutes.
In 10 (1-pint) hot sterilized jars, divide the soup, leaving about ½-inch space from the top.
Run a knife around the insides of each jar to remove any air bubbles.
Wipe any trace of food off the rims of jars with a clean, moist kitchen towel.
Carefully place the jars in the pressure canner and process at 10 pounds pressure for about 75 minutes.
Take the jars out from the pressure canner and place them onto a wood surface several inches apart to cool completely. After cooling with your finger, press the top of each jar's lid to ensure that the seal is tight.
Store these canning jars in a cool, dark place.

Nutrition: Calories: 279.8; Fat: 3.8g; Carbs: 34.1g; Fiber: 8.5g; Sugar: 4.5g; Protein: 27.4g

55. Homemade Canned Pork

Preparation Time: 1 hour
Curing Time: 2 days
Canning Time: 70 minutes
Servings: 3 jars

Ingredients:

- Pounds pork butt (fat trimmed off)
- ½ teaspoon cure
- 1 ½ teaspoon kosher salt
- ½ teaspoon allspice
- ½ teaspoon black pepper
- garlic 1 clove (minced or pressed)
- 3 bay leaves (1 per jar)
- 3 tablespoons caramelized onion (1 tablespoon per jar)

Directions: Cut the pork meat into 1-inch pieces. Mix the cure with the salt. Place the meat into a bowl, sprinkle with the salt-cure mixture, and mix well. Cover the bowl and keep it in a refrigerator for 24 to 48 hours.
Take out the meat after the curing process, add in the allspice, black peppers, garlic, and mix well. Pack the meat into 16-ounce jars, leaving ½ in. of headspace. Add one bay leaf and a tablespoon of caramelized onion to each jar. Wipe the rims, place the lids on top, and screw on the bands finger-tight. Put the jars in a pressure canner and process them at 15 PSI (250°F) for 70 minutes.
Remove the container from heat and allow it to naturally depressurize. Use a jar lifter to remove the jars and put them on a towel-lined counter to cool down at room temperature for about 12 hours.
Remove the bands, wipe the jars, and test the seals. Store in a cool, dark, and dry place for up to 2–3 years.

Nutrition: Carbs: 1.9g; Fat: 18.8g; Fiber: 0.8g; Sugar: 0.9g; Protein: 63.1g; Calories: 448.5

56. Canned Beef Stroganoff

Preparation Time: 30 minutes
Canning Time: 75 minutes
Cooking Time: 40 minutes
Servings: 6

Ingredients:

- 1 teaspoon black pepper
- 2 teaspoons salt
- 2 teaspoons thyme
- 2 teaspoons parsley
- 4 tablespoons Worcestershire sauce
- 2 garlic cloves, minced
- 1 cup mushrooms, sliced
- 1 cup onion, chopped
- 2 pounds stewing beef, cut into chunks
- 4 cups beef broth

Directions: Sterilize the bottles in a pressure canner as indicated in the general guidelines. Allow the bottles to cool. Place all the needed ingredients in a pot and bring to a boil for 10 minutes. Reduce the heat and allow simmering for another 30 minutes. Turn off the heat and allow cooling slightly.
Transfer the mixture to sterilized bottles. Remove air bubbles and close the jars.
Put the jars in a pressure canner and process for 75 minutes.

Nutrition: Calories: 149.8; Fat: 7.9g; Fiber: 1.8g; Carbs: 7.9g; Protein: 24.1g

57. Canned Chili

Preparation Time: 15 minutes
Canning Time: 75 minutes
Cooking Time: 30 minutes
Servings: 6

Ingredients:

- 3 cups dry kidney beans, soaked overnight and drained
- 2 pounds ground beef
- 1 cup onion, chopped
- 1 cup pepper, seeded and chopped
- 4 cups tomatoes, chopped
- 1 tablespoon chili pepper, seeded and chopped

Directions: Sterilize the bottles in a pressure canner as indicated in the general guidelines. Allow the bottles to cool. Place the beans in a pot and boil for 30 minutes. Drain the beans.
To a clean pot, put the cooked beans and the rest of the ingredients. Cook for another 20 minutes.
Transfer the mixture into the sterilized bottles. Leave an inch of headspace.
Remove air bubbles and close jars.
Place the jars in a pressure canner and process for 75 minutes. Follow the guidelines for pressure canning.

Nutrition: Calories: 162.8; Fat: 7.9g; Fiber: 1.8g; Carbs: 7.7g; Protein: 11.2g

58. Ground Beef, Pork, Lamb, or Sausage

Preparation Time: 10 minutes
Canning Time: 1 hour and 15 minutes
Cooking Time: 20 minutes
Servings: 2

Ingredients:
- Preferred meat, fresh, chilled, chopped/ground
- Salt (1 teaspoon for each quart jar)
- 3 cups Meat broth, boiling/tomato juice/water

Directions: Chop the chilled fresh meat into small chunks. If using venison, grind after mixing with one cup of pork fat (high quality) to every three to four cups of venison. If using sausage (freshly made), combine with cayenne pepper and salt.

Shape into meatballs or patties. If using cased sausage, chop into three to four-inch links.

Cook the meat until light brown. If using ground meat, sauté without shaping.

Add the cooked meat to clean and hot Mason jars. Each filled with salt (1 teaspoon).

Boil the meat broth. Pour the meat broth, tomato juice, or water into the jars until filled up to one inch from the top. Remove air bubbles before adjusting the lids, then process in the pressure canner for 1 hour and 15 minutes (pints) or 1 hour and 30 minutes (quarts).

Nutrition: Calories: 599.8; Fat: 7.9g; Fiber: 1.8g; Carbs: 7.9g; Protein: 6.2g

59. Meat Stock

Preparation Time: 10 minutes
Canning Time: 20 minutes/75 minutes
Cooking Time: +1 hour
Servings: 2

Ingredients:
- 4 Beef/chicken bones
- 4 cups, Water

Directions: If making beef broth:

After cracking the beef bones (fresh trimmed), rinse and place in a stockpot filled with enough water to cover the bones. Heat until boiling then allow it to simmer for about 3 to 4 hours.

Discard the bones and let the broth cool before skimming excess fat. Reheat the broth and then pour into clean and hot Mason jars, each with a one-inch headspace remaining.

Adjust the lids after removing air bubbles and process in the pressure canner for 20 minutes (pints) or 25 minutes (quarts). If making chicken/turkey broth:

Fill a large stockpot with your large chicken or turkey bones. Pour some water into it, enough to cover the bones, then cover and simmer for 30 to 45 minutes.

Discard the bones and let the broth cool before removing excess fat. Reheat before pouring into clean and hot Mason jars, each left with one-inch headspace.

Adjust the jar lids before processing in the pressure canner for 75 minutes (for pint jars) or 90 minutes (for quart jars).

Nutrition: Calories: 599.9; Fat: 7.7g; Fiber: 1.6g; Carbs: 7.9g; Protein: 6.2g

60. Chili with Beef

Preparation Time: 10 minutes
Canning Time: 1 hour and 25 minutes
Cooking Time: 35 minutes
Servings: 2

Ingredients:
- 5 ½ cups water
- 2 quarts tomatoes, whole/crushed
- 1 cup peppers, chopped
- 3 pounds beef, ground
- 5 tablespoons chili powder
- 3 cups red kidney/pinto beans, dried
- 5 teaspoons salt divided
- 1 ½ cups onions, chopped
- 1 teaspoon black pepper

Directions: Thoroughly wash the beans before adding them to a saucepan (2-quart). Cover with cold water and let sit for 12 hours.

Drain the beans that have been soaked and place them in a saucepan filled with fresh water (5 ½ cups) and salt (2 teaspoons). Stir to combine and heat until boiling, then simmer for half an hour.

Drain the cooked beans and then return to the saucepan. Stir in salt (3 teaspoons), chili powder, pepper, and tomatoes. Simmer the mixture for 5 minutes; avoid letting the mixture thicken.

Pour the mixture into clean and hot Mason jars, each with a one-inch headspace remaining. Get rid of any air bubbles before adjusting the jar lids. Put in the pressure canner and process for 1 hour and 25 minutes.

Nutrition: Calories: 199.8; Fat: 7.8g; Fiber: 1.8g; Carbs: 7.9g; Protein: 6.2g

61. Beef in Wine Sauce

Preparation Time: 20 minutes
Canning Time: 1 ¼ hour
Cooking Time: 2 hours and 20 minutes
Servings: 6

Ingredients:

- 1 tablespoon vegetable oil
- 2 pounds beef stew meat, cut into 1-inch cubes
- 1 cup carrot, peeled and shredded
- ¾ cup onion, sliced
- 1 large apple; peeled, cored, and shredded
- 2 garlic cloves, minced
- ¾ cup water
- ½ cup red wine
- 2 beef bouillon cubes
- 2 bay leaves
- 1 teaspoon salt

Directions: In a cast-iron wok, heat vegetable oil over medium-high heat and sear beef cubes in 2 batches for about 4–5 minutes and then add in the remaining ingredients and mix well.
Now adjust the heat to high and bring to a full rolling boil.
Now set the heat to low and cook, covered for about 1 hour, stirring occasionally.
Remove the wok of meat mixture from the heat and discard the bay leaves.
In 3 (1-pint) hot sterilized jars, divide the beef mixture, leaving about 1-inch space from the top.
Run a knife around the insides of each jar to remove any air bubbles.
Remove all traces of food off the rims of jars with a clean, moist kitchen towel.
Close each jar with a lid and screw on the ring.
Carefully place the jars in the pressure canner and process at 10 pounds pressure for about 75 minutes.
Remove the jars from the pressure canner and place them onto a wood surface several inches apart to cool completely. After cooling with your finger, press the top of each jar's lid to ensure that the seal is tight.
Store these canning jars in a cool, dark place.

Nutrition: Calories: 353.8; Fat: 11.7g; Carbs: 9.1g; Fiber: 1.5g; Sugar: 5.6g; Protein: 46.8g

62. Beef Meatballs

Preparation Time: 20 minutes
Canning Time: 1 ¼ hour
Cooking Time: 15 minutes
Servings: 16

Ingredients:

- 6 pounds ground beef
- 6 cups soft bread crumbs
- 6 large eggs
- 1 ½ cups water
- 1 cup onion, chopped finely
- 1 tablespoon salt
- ¼ teaspoon ground black pepper
- 8 cups hot chicken broth

Directions: In a glass bowl, add all ingredients (except for broth) and mix until just combined.
Set aside for about 15–30 minutes. Preheat your oven to 425°F.
Lightly grease 2 shallow baking dishes. Make 1-inch balls from the mixture.
Arrange the meatballs onto the prepared baking dishes in a single layer.
Bake for approximately 15 minutes. In 8 (1-pint) hot sterilized jars, divide the meatballs.
Now pack each jar with hot broth, leaving 1-inch space from the top.
Run a knife around the insides of each jar to remove any air bubbles.
Remove all trace of food off the rims of jars with a clean, moist kitchen towel.
Close each jar with a lid and screw on the ring.
Carefully place the jars in the pressure canner and process at 10 pounds pressure for about 75 minutes.
Take the jars out of the pressure canner and place them onto a wood surface several inches apart to cool completely. After cooling with your finger, press the top of each jar's lid to ensure that the seal is tight.
Store these canning jars in a cool, dark place.

Nutrition: Calories: 524.8; Fat: 15.1g; Carbs: 30.1g; Fiber: 1.9g; Sugar: 3.2g; Protein: 62.1g

63. Ham

Preparation Time: 15 minutes
Canning Time: 1 ¼ hour
Cooking Time: 40 minutes
Servings: 40

Ingredients:

- 19 pounds ham, cut into ½-inch chunks

Directions: Heat a lightly greased large cast-iron skillet over medium-high heat and sear ham chunks in 8 batches for about 3–5 minutes. In 10 (1-pint) hot sterilized jars, divide the ham chunks.
Now pack each jar with hot water, leaving 1-inch space from the top.

Run a knife around the insides of each jar to remove any air bubbles.
Remove all trace of food off the rims of jars with a clean, moist kitchen towel.
Close each jar with a lid and screw on the ring.
Carefully place the jars in the pressure canner and process at 11 pounds pressure for about 75 minutes.
Remove the jars from the pressure canner and place them onto a wood surface several inches apart to cool completely.
After cooling with your finger, press the top of each jar's lid to ensure that the seal is tight.
Store these canning jars in a cool, dark place.

Nutrition: Calories: 350.8; Fat: 18.3g; Carbs: 8.1g; Fiber: 2.7g; Sugar: 0g; Protein: 35.9g

64. Ground Beef in Tomato Sauce

Preparation Time: 20 minutes
Canning Time: 1 hour
Cooking Time: 55 minutes
Servings: 18

Ingredients:
- 30 pounds tomatoes
- 2 pounds ground beef
- 1 cup onions, chopped
- 1 cup celery, chopped
- 1 pound fresh mushrooms, sliced
- 5 garlic cloves, minced
- 2 tablespoons oregano, minced
- 2 tablespoons parsley, minced
- ¼ cup brown sugar
- 1 ½ tablespoon salt
- 2 teaspoons ground black pepper
- Boiling water

Directions: In the saucepan of boiling water, cook the tomatoes for about 30–60 seconds.
Remove from heat and transfer the tomatoes into a bowl of cold water. Carefully remove the skins and cores.
Then, chop the tomatoes roughly. In a pan of water, boil tomatoes for about 20 minutes.
Through a food mill, pass the tomatoes. Heat a cast-iron skillet and cook the beef for about 8–10 minutes.
Add onion, celery, mushrooms, and garlic and cook for about 4–5 minutes.
Transfer the vegetable mixture into the pan with tomato pulp.
Add herbs, sugar, salt, and black pepper and cook until boiling.
Now set the heat to low and cook, uncovered, for about 5–10 minutes, stirring frequently.
In 9 (1-pint) hot sterilized jars, divide the beef mixture, leaving about 1-inch space from the top.
Run a knife around the insides of each jar to remove any air bubbles.
Remove all trace of food off the rims of jars with a clean, moist kitchen towel.
Close each jar with a lid and screw on the ring.
Carefully place the jars in the pressure canner and process at 10 pounds pressure for about 60 minutes.
Remove the jars from the pressure canner and place them onto a wood surface several inches apart to cool completely. After cooling with your finger, press the top of each jar's lid to ensure that the seal is tight.
Store these canning jars in a cool, dark place.

Nutrition: Calories: 249.8; Fat: 4.6g; Carbs: 33.5g; Fiber: 9.7g; Sugar: 22.5g; Protein: 23.2g

65. Canned Venison

Preparation Time: 20 minutes
Servings: 6
Canning Time: 1 hour and 30 minutes

Ingredients:
- 4 Oz, Fresh venison meat
- 2 tsp., Canning salt

Directions: Preheat your pressure canner. Slice your meat across the grain, into strips or chunks of whatever size you prefer.
Pack the meat into hot jars, leaving about 1 inch at the top. Add 1 tablespoon of canning salt per quart that your jar holds. So, if you're packing meat into a 4-quart jar, you'll add 4 tablespoons of salt.
Use a spatula or the back of a spoon to force out air bubbles before you screw the lid on and affix the band.
Place your jars in the pressure canner and make sure there's at least 1 inch of space between them. They shouldn't touch one another.
Process in your canner for an hour and a half. Remove your jars and allow them to cool.

Nutrition: Calories: 442.8; Fat: 7.9g; Fiber: 0.9g; Carbs: 7.8g; Protein: 3.2g

66. Smoky Meatloaf

Preparation Time: 20 minutes **Canning Time:** 1 ¼ hour
Servings: 16

Ingredients:
- ¼ French bread loaf
- 5 pounds ground beef
- 1 onion, chopped
- 4 large eggs
- 1½ cups ketchup
- 2 tablespoons Worcestershire sauce
- ¾ cup brown sugar
- 2 tablespoons salt
- 1 tablespoon powdered smoke
- 1 tablespoon sage
- 1 tablespoon garlic powder
- ½ tablespoon onion salt
- ½ tablespoon ground black pepper

Directions: Add bread loaf into a food processor and process until crumbed.
In a large glass bowl, add bread crumbs and the remaining ingredients and mix until well combined.
In 8 (1-pint) hot sterilized jars, divide the beef mixture, leaving about 1-inch space from the top.
Run a knife around the insides of each jar to remove any air bubbles.
Wipe any trace of food off the rims of jars with a clean, moist kitchen towel.
Close each jar with a lid and screw on the ring.
Carefully place the jars in the pressure canner and process at 10 pounds pressure for about 75 minutes.
Remove the jars from the pressure canner and place them onto a wood surface several inches apart to cool completely. After cooling with your finger, press the top of each jar's lid to ensure that the seal is tight.
Store these canning jars in a cool, dark place.

Nutrition: Calories: 346.9; Fat: 10.2g; Carbs: 16.1g; Fiber: 0.3g; Sugar: 12.5g; Protein: 45.7g

67. Chicken Soup

Preparation Time: 30 minutes **Cooking Time:** 30 minutes
Canning Time: 1 hour and 15 minutes **Servings:** 8-pint jars

Ingredients:
- 3 cups chicken (diced)
- 6 cups chicken broth
- 10 cups water
- 1 cup onion (diced)
- Salt and pepper to taste
- 1 ½ cups celery (diced)
- 1 ½ cups carrots (sliced)
- 3 chicken bouillon cubes

Directions: Sterilize the jars.
Mix all the ingredients in a pot except the salt, pepper, and bouillon cubes and bring to boil.
Reduce the flame and simmer for 30 minutes.
Stir in the remaining ingredients and stir cook until the bouillon cubes dissolve.
Turn off the flame and remove any visible foam.
Ladle the mix immediately into the sterilized jars, leaving 1 inch of headspace.
Get rid of any air bubbles and clean the rims.
Cover the jars with the lid and apply the bands making sure that it is tightened.
Process the jars for 1 hour 15 minutes at 10 pounds pressure in a pressure canner.
Remove; allow cooling, and then label the jars.

Nutrition: Calories: 75.2; Fat: 0.2g; Carbs: 5.1g; Proteins: 12.4g

68. Canned Chicken

Preparation Time: 30 minutes **Cooking Time:** 10 minutes
Canning Time: 70 minutes **Servings:** 8-pint jars

Ingredients:
- 18 medium boneless and skinless chicken breasts
- 1 ½ tablespoon salt
- 4 ½ cups water
- Butter or Olive Oil for frying in a skillet

Directions: Cook each side of the chicken in a skillet with some butter or olive oil, about 8–10 minutes. Remove from heat when the chicken is white and cooked all the way through. If you poke it with a fork, the juices run clear.
In each pint jar, place ½ teaspoon of salt and 2 chicken breasts.
Fill the jar with water, process for 70 minutes at 10 pounds of pressure for the weighted gauge of the pressure canner or 11 pounds if the pressure canner has a dial gauge.
Remove the jars, and let them cool until it is room temperature, which may take about a day.

Nutrition: Carbs: 0g; Fat: 54.8g; Protein: 5.2g; Calories: 508.7

69. Mexican Turkey Soup

Preparation Time: 20 minutes
Canning Time: 90 minutes
Cooking Time: 20 minutes
Servings: 8-quart jars or 16-pint jars

Ingredients:
- 6 cups cooked turkey, chopped
- 2 cups chopped onions
- 8-ounce can of Mexican green chilies, chopped and drained
- ¼ cup taco seasoning mix, packed
- 28 ounces crushed tomatoes with the juices
- 16 cups turkey or chicken broth
- 3 cups corn
- 1 ½ tablespoon extra-virgin olive oil

Directions: In a large stockpot, warm olive oil on medium-high heat. Sauté the onions until tender and fragrant, about 2 minutes on medium-high heat. Reduce the heat to medium-low.
Add taco seasoning and chilies. Cook and stir for another 3 minutes, add in the tomatoes and the broth. Bring to a boil, and then add the corn and the turkey. Reduce the heat to low, and let simmer for 10 minutes.
Ladle equally into the jars.
Process pints at 10 pounds for 75 minutes and quarts at 10 pounds for 90 minutes for the weighted gauge of the pressure canner or 11 pounds if the pressure canner has a dial gauge.
Remove the jars, and let them cool until it is at room temperature. This may take about a day.

Nutrition: Carbs: 29.8g; Fat: 76.6g; Protein: 63.8g; Calories: 1078.8

70. Pineapple Chicken

Preparation Time: 15 minutes
Canning Time: 90 minutes
Cooking Time: 10 minutes
Servings: 4

Ingredients:
- 3 cups pineapple juice
- ¾ cup brown sugar
- 1 ¼ cups apple cider vinegar
- 6 tablespoons soy sauce
- 4 tablespoons tomato paste
- 1 teaspoon ground ginger
- 4 minced garlic cloves
- 5 pounds chopped boneless and skinless chicken
- 2 diced onions
- 3 diced bell peppers
- 1 diced pineapple
- Crushed chili pepper, to taste

Directions: In a sizable saucepan, bring to a boil pineapple juice, sugar, vinegar, soy sauce, tomato paste, ginger, and garlic, stirring frequently. Boil for the sugar to dissolve and until the mixture is smooth.
In your jars, layer chicken, onions, peppers, and pineapple. If you're using crushed chilies, add them now.
Put the sauce over the contents of the jars.
Wipe the rims of the jars, put the lids on, and process in a pressure canner at 11 PSI for 90 minutes, adjusting for altitude.

Nutrition: Calories: 107.9; Fat: 49.8g; Fiber: 1.9g; Carbs: 7.9g; Protein: 48.3g

71. Chicken Breast

Preparation Time: 15 minutes
Servings: 5 pints
Canning Time: 75 minutes

Ingredients:
- 5 pounds chicken breast
- 1tsp. Salt

Directions: Cut the chicken into small pieces that will fit into the jars. Place the chicken in the sterilized jars leaving 1-inch headspace.
Add a 1/2 tablespoon of salt to each jar. (You may add water, but chicken makes its juice.)
Get rid of the air bubbles and wipe the jar rims with a damp cloth.
Put the lids and the rings on the jars. Transfer the jars to the pressure canner and process them at 10 pounds pressure for 75 minutes.
Wait for the pressure canner to depressurize to zero before removing the jars.
Put the jars on a cooling rack for 24 hours, then store them in a cool, dry place.

Nutrition: Calories: 107.9; Fat: 49.7g; Fiber: 1.8g; Carbs: 7.9g; Protein: 48.2g

72. Rosemary Chicken

Preparation Time: 15 minutes
Servings: 10 pints
Canning Time: 75 minutes

Ingredients:
- 20 (2-inch) sprigs of rosemary
- 10 pounds chicken breast, boneless and skinless
- ¼ cup salt

Directions: Add a sprig of rosemary to each sterilized jar.
Cut the chicken breasts into large chunks and pack in the jars, leaving a 1–1/2 inches headspace.
Put a sprig of rosemary at the top, then add a tablespoon of salt to each jar.
Clean the rims of the jar with a clean damp towel, and then place the lids and the rings. Transfer the jars to the pressure canner and process them at 10 pounds pressure for 75 minutes.
Wait for the pressure canner to depressurize to zero before removing the jars using cooking tongs
Put the jars on a cooling rack for 24 hours to seal, then store them in a cool, dry place.

Nutrition: Calories: 107.9; Fat: 49.9g; Fiber: 1.8g; Carbs: 7.9g; Protein: 48.2g

73. Canned Turkey Pieces

Preparation Time: 15 minutes
Canning Time: 75 minutes
Cooking Time: 15 minutes
Servings: 5 pints

Ingredients:
- 5 pounds turkey
- Boiling water

Directions: Cook the turkey meat until it is 2/3 cooked.
Pack the turkey pieces in the sterilized jars, then add water or stock, leaving 1-inch headspace.
Remove the air bubbles. Wipe the rims with a damp cloth.
Put the lids and the rings on the jars. Transfer the jars to the pressure canner and process them at 10 pounds pressure for 65 minutes if the turkey had bones and 75 minutes if without bones.
Wait for the pressure canner to depressurize to zero before removing the jars.
Put the jars on a cooling rack for 24 hours, then store them in a cool, dry place.

Nutrition: Calories: 107.8; Fat: 49.7g; Fiber: 1.8g; Carbs: 7.8g; Protein: 48.2g

74. Turkey and Green Beans

Preparation Time: 15 minutes
Canning Time: 90 minutes
Cooking Time: 10 minutes
Servings: 4 pints

Ingredients:
- 4 cups shredded cooked turkey
- 2 cups cut green beans
- 1 ½ cups chopped carrots
- 1 cup sliced onion
- 2 cups chicken or turkey broth
- 3 quarts water
- 2 tablespoons distilled white vinegar

Directions: In a small stockpot, combine the turkey, green beans, carrots, onion, and broth. Bring to a boil over medium-high heat. Let it cook for 5 minutes, then remove it from the fire. Arrange the hot jars on a cutting board. Ladle the hot mixture using a funnel into the jars, leaving some headspace. Eliminate any air bubbles and add additional mixture if necessary. Rinse the rim of each jar with a warm cloth dipped in white vinegar.
Add 3 quarts of water and add 2 tablespoons of distilled white vinegar into the pressure canner.
Put the jars in the pressure canner, lock the pressure canner lid, and bring to a boil over high heat for 10 minutes.
Process for 90 minutes (quarts) and 75 minutes (pints).
Let the pressure in the canner reach zero, then remove the jars after 10 minutes.

Nutrition: Calories: 107.9; Fat: 49.9g; Fiber: 1.8g; Carbs: 7.7g; Protein: 48.2g

75. Turkey Sausage

Preparation Time: 15 minutes
Canning Time: 1 hour and 30 minutes
Cooking Time: 10 minutes
Servings: 4 pints

Ingredients:
- ½ cup warm water
- 2 teaspoons dried basil
- 2 teaspoons rubbed sage

- 2 teaspoons red pepper flakes
- 1 ½ teaspoons marjoram
- 1 teaspoon dried mustard
- ½ teaspoon ground thyme
- ½ teaspoon coarse sea salt
- ½ teaspoon ground black pepper
- 1 teaspoon garlic powder
- 1 teaspoon paprika
- 3 pounds ground turkey
- ½ cup grapeseed or extra-virgin olive oil

Directions: Combine the basil, sage, red pepper flakes, marjoram, mustard, thyme, salt, pepper, garlic powder, and paprika in a large mixing bowl. Combine the ground turkey and all of the spices in a clean bowl with your hands. Return the turkey to the bowl by rolling it into a big ball.

Using your hands, evenly pour oil over the whole surface of the turkey meatball, raising and rotating the ball to coat. Return the turkey ball to the mixing basin. Refrigerate the bowl overnight or for 12 hours after covering it with plastic wrap.

Form the turkey into patties or links, or leave it unformed in a skillet, brown patties, or links on both sides for approximately 1 minute each. In a pan, loose brown sausage for approximately 10 minutes. Before filling jars, drain any extra oil using whatever technique you prefer.

Place the meat in heated jars with a headspace of 114 inches. Using a warm towel soaked in distilled white vinegar, wipe the rims of each jar. Hand-tighten the lids and rings on each jar.

Fill the pressure canner halfway with water, seal the top, and bring to a boil over high heat. Allow 10 minutes for the canner to vent. Close the vent and keep heating until the dial gauge reaches 11 PSI and the weighted gauge reaches 10 PSI. 1 hour 30 minutes for quart jars and 1 hour 15 minutes for pint jars.

Nutrition: Calories: 149.8; Fat: 7.9g; Fiber: 1.6g; Carbs: 7.8g; Protein: 24.1g

76. Chili with Beef (2nd Version)

Preparation Time: 15 minutes
Canning Time: 75 minutes
Cooking Time: 35 minutes
Servings: 9 pints

Ingredients:
- 3 cups dried red kidney beans
- 5 ½ cups water
- 5 teaspoons salt, divided
- 3 pounds ground beef
- 1 ½ cups onions, chopped
- 1 cup red bell peppers, chopped
- 1 teaspoon black pepper
- 4 tablespoons chili powder
- 2 quarts crushed tomatoes

Directions: In a large pot, combine the beans with water and salt.
Bring the pot to a boil, reduce the heat, and cook for 30 minutes and then drain.
In a large skillet, lightly brown the ground beef, along with the onions and peppers, and drain.
Pour into a large pot and add some salt, pepper, chili powder, tomatoes, and beans.
Let this mixture simmer for at least 5 minutes. Pour the chili into sterile jars, leaving 1-inch headspace.
Wipe the jar rims clean and adjust the lids.
Process the jars in a pressure canner for 75 minutes at 10 pounds of pressure for a pressure canner with a weighted gauge (or 11 pounds if the pressure canner has a dial gauge).

Nutrition: Calories: 339.87; Fat: 7.9g; Fiber: 1.8g; Carbs: 7.9g; Protein: 6.2g

77. Chicken with Garlic

Preparation Time: 15 minutes
Servings: 3
Canning Time: 90 minutes

Ingredients:
- 1 crushed garlic clove
- 3 skinless, boneless chicken breasts
- ½ teaspoons sea salt
- ½ teaspoons black pepper
- Water, as needed

Directions: Put part of the garlic clove at the bottom of each sanitized quart jar.
Add chicken pieces, pushing them down to pack tightly.
Add salt and pepper, and then fill the jar with water, allowing 1 inch of headspace.
Carefully slide a rubber spatula utensil down the interior sides of the jars, removing air pockets. Do not skip this step, or your jars may not seal. Wipe the rims of the jars.
Process a pressure canner for 90 minutes at 10 PSI, adjusting for altitude with the lids on.

Nutrition: Calories: 339.8; Fat: 7.9g; Fiber: 1.8g; Carbs: 7.9g; Protein: 6.2g

78. Venison

Preparation Time: 15 minutes **Cooking Time: 1 hour & 20 minutes**
Servings: 5 pints

Ingredients:
- 5 lbs. cubed venison
- 1 tbsp. vinegar
- broth
- Cajun seasoning
- Canning salt
- Paper towels
- 1 box of beef

Directions: Align a canning rack in the bottom of a 12-quart pressure canner. Fill each jar halfway with meat. Add ½ teaspoon of canning salt and ¼ tsp Cajun seasoning.
Leave 1 inch from the top. Add 1 tablespoon of beef broth. Wipe rim of jar clean.
Heat lids in hot water for 3 minutes; place lids on jars and tighten rings on slightly. Transfer the jars into the canner and fill with water up to the jar rings; add vinegar to the water.
Close and lock the pressure canner and bring to a boil over high heat, then add cooking weight to the top.
After 20 minutes, adjust the heat to medium and cook for 75 minutes. Turn off heat and leave the canner alone until it has cooled completely to room temperature.
After it has cooled, remove the jars from the canner and check for sealing. If jars have sealed, store for up to 2 years; if not, use the meat right away.

Nutrition: Calories: 146.8; Fat: 1.9g; Carbs: 0g; Protein: 27.2g

79. Canned Roast Beef

Preparation Time: 30 minutes **Cooking Time: 20 minutes**
Canning Time: 1 hour and 30 minutes **Servings: 9 pints**

Ingredients:
- 3 pounds chuck roast, cubed
- 1 large onion, cut into eighths
- 1 ½ teaspoons salt

Directions: Preheat your pressure canner.
Pack the meat into 4 hot jars, add the onion in each of the jars followed by ½ teaspoon of salt per pound of meat, leaving about 1 inch of space at the top.
Use a spatula or the back of a spoon to force out air bubbles before you screw the lid on and affix the band.
Place the jars in the pressure canner and process for an hour and a half. Remove the jars and allow them to cool.

Nutrition: Calories: 554.8; Fat: 27.9g; Fiber: 1.9g; Carbs: 5.8g; Protein: 67.2g

80. Chicken Soup

Preparation Time: 20 minutes **Cooking Time: 20 minutes**
Canning Time: 1 hour and 30 minutes **Servings: 9 pints**

Ingredients:
- 6 quarts chicken broth
- 6 cups cooked chicken
- 2 cups celery, chopped
- 2 cups carrots, chopped
- 1 cup onions, chopped
- 1 cup mushrooms, sliced
- 2 garlic cloves
- 1 tablespoon salt
- 1 teaspoon pepper

Directions: In a large stockpot, heat the broth and the chicken.
Add celery, carrots, onions, mushrooms, and garlic. Bring the mixture to a boil. Add salt and pepper.
Use a slotted spoon to grab the solid parts of the soup and place into hot jars.
Add the cooking liquid on top, and leave about 1 inch of space at the top of the jars.
Place the lids and bands on the jars and process in your pressure canner for an hour and a half.
Remove and allow jars to cool.

Nutrition: Calories: 554.8; Fat: 27.9g; Fiber: 1.7g; Carbs: 5.8g; Protein: 67.2g

81. Canned Lamb

Preparation Time: 15 minutes **Cooking Time: 1 hour & 35 minutes**
Servings: 5

Ingredients:
- 5 lbs. cubed lamb

- 5-pint sized mason jars with lids and rings
- Canning salt

Directions: Fill jars with meat to 1 inch from the top. Add ½ tsp canning salt per pint. Pour hot water over meat and salt. Use a knife to jiggle the meat and remove any air pockets. Wipe rim of jar clean.
Heat lids in hot water for 3 minutes; place lids on jars and tighten rings slightly. Arrange the jars in the canner and fill with water up to the jar rings; add vinegar to the water.
Close and lock the pressure canner and bring to a boil over high heat, then add cooking weight to the top. After 20 minutes, reduce the heat to medium and cook for 75 minutes.
Turn off your heat and leave the canner alone until it has cooled completely to room temperature. After the canner has cooled, remove the jars from the canner and check for sealing.
If jars have sealed, store for up to 2 years; if not, use the meat right away.

Nutrition: Calories: 257.8; Fat: 16.3g; Carbs: 0g; Protein: 25.8g

82. Beef Stroganoff with Mushroom

Preparation Time: 15 minutes **Cooking Time: 1 hour & 40 minutes**
Servings: 1

Ingredients:
- 5 lbs. chopped beef
- 2 chopped onions
- 4 chopped garlic cloves
- 4 cups sliced mushrooms
- 1 tbsp. butter
- 2 tbsps. Worcestershire sauce
- Water, as needed
- Salt and pepper, to taste

Directions: Fry the beef, onions, garlic, and mushrooms in butter in a sizable saucepan until a brown color. Mix in Worcestershire sauce, seasonings, and enough water as you stir to deglaze the stockpot.
Pour 2 more cups of water as you stir, then leave to boil. Ladle the stroganoff into sanitized quart jars, distributing the cooking liquid evenly across the jars. Do not worry about adding more liquid—when the meat cooks, it will add flavorful juices. Process in your pressure canner for 90 minutes at 10 PSI, adjusting for altitude.

Nutrition: Calories: 244.1; Fat: 8.1g; Carbs: 11.1g; Protein: 31.5g

83. Canned Tilapia

Preparation Time: 15 minutes **Cooking Time: 1 hour & 25 minutes**
Servings: 5 pints

Ingredients:
- 5 lbs. tilapia fillets
- Canning salt
- Lemon juice
- 1 jalapeño pepper

Directions: Place 1 slice of jalapeño pepper into each jar. Fill jars with fish to ½ inch from the top. Add ¼-teaspoon of canning salt and 1 tsp lemon juice per pint.
Use a knife to jiggle the meat and remove any air pockets. Wipe rim of jar clean. Heat lids in hot water for 3 minutes; place lids on jars and tighten rings slightly.
Arrange the jars in the canner and fill with water up to the jar rings. Close and lock the pressure canner and bring to a boil over high heat, then add cooking weight to the top.
After 20 minutes, adjust the heat to medium and cook for 75 minutes. Turn off the heat and leave the canner alone until it has cooled completely to room temperature.
After canner has cooled, remove the jars from the canner and check for sealing. If jars have sealed, store for up to 2 years; if not, use the meat right away.

Nutrition: Calories: 95.8; Fat: 1.5g; Carbs: 0g; Protein: 20.2g

84. Canned Chicken Pieces

Preparation Time: 15 minutes **Cooking Time: 1 hour & 20 minutes**
Servings: 10 pints

Ingredients:
- Dry chicken bouillon granules
- 20 lbs. of fresh chicken pieces
- Canning salt

Directions: Remove fat from chicken. Chop chicken into cubed pieces, if desired. Place canning jars into the dishwasher and run through without any detergent to warm the jars.

Heat 3 quarts of water for your pressure canner to almost boiling. Heat lids in hot water for 3 minutes.
Add ½ teaspoon of canning salt and ½ tsp chicken bouillon granules to the bottom of each canning jar. Place chicken into canning jars with one inch of space at the top.
Place lids on and tighten rings. Place jars into the canner and fill with hot water to the jar rings.
Close and lock the pressure canner and bring to a boil over high heat, then add cooking weight to the top.
After 15 minutes, turn the heat to medium and cook for 75 minutes. Turn off your heat and leave the canner alone until it has cooled completely to room temperature.
After the canner has cooled, remove the jars from the canner and check for sealing.

Nutrition: Calories: 230.8; Fat: 9.8g; Carbs: 1.2g; Protein: 32.2g

85. Canned Turkey Meat

Preparation Time: 15 minutes
Servings: 10 pints
Cooking Time: 1 hour & 20 minutes

Ingredients:
- *Dry chicken bouillon granules*
- *15 lb. fresh whole turkey or turkey pieces (not frozen)*
- *Canning salt*

Directions: If using a whole turkey, cut into manageable pieces. Place canning jars into the dishwasher and run through, without any detergent, to warm the jars.
Heat 3 quarts of water for your pressure canner to not quite boiling. Heat lids in hot water for 3 minutes.
Add ½ teaspoon of canning salt and ½ tsp chicken bouillon granules to the bottom of each canning jar. Place turkey into the canning jars with one inch of space at the top.
Place lids on and tighten rings. Place jars into the canner and fill with hot water to the jar rings.
Close and lock the pressure canner and bring to a boil over high heat, then add cooking weight to the top. After 15 minutes, turn the heat to medium and cook for 75 minutes.
Turn off the heat and leave the canner alone until it has cooled completely to room temperature.   After it has cooled, remove the jars from the canner and check for sealing.

Nutrition: Calories: 239.8; Fat: 9.6g; Carbs: 1.9g; Protein: 33.8g

86. Canned Chili

Preparation Time: 15 minutes
Servings: 12 pints
Cooking Time: 1 hour & 50 minutes

Ingredients:
- *3 cups kidney beans*
- *5 tbsps. salt*
- *3 lbs. beef, ground*
- *1 ½ cups chopped onion*
- *1 cup chopped bell peppers*
- *6 tbsps. chili seasoning mix*
- *1 tbsp. black pepper*
- *8 cups chopped tomatoes*
- *4 cups tomato juice*
- *15 oz. tomato sauce*

Directions: Wash beans in clean water and rinse them. Put the beans in a stockpot and cover them with water, 2 inches above the beans. Let the beans soak overnight.
Rinse the beans and add more water with 2 tablespoons salt. Heat the beans and water until simmering, then cook for 30 minutes. Drain the beans.
Brown onions, beef, and bell peppers in a large skillet. Transfer them to a large pot, then add the beans.
Add seasoning mix, black pepper, tomatoes, tomato sauce, and tomato juice to the pot and simmer for 5 minutes.
Ladle the mixture to the sterilized jars leaving a 1-inch headspace. Wipe the rims and place the lid and rings on the jars.
Process the jars at 11 pounds of pressure for 75 minutes. Wait for the canner to cool to remove the jars. Place the jars on a cooling rack until the lids seal

Nutrition: Calories: 451.8; Fat: 14.9g; Carbs: 39.7g; Protein: 43.2g

87. Chicken Jambalaya with Sausage

Preparation Time: 15 minutes
Servings: 1 quart
Cooking Time: 1 hour & 50 minutes

Ingredients:
- *1 tbsp. olive oil*
- *4-lbs. cubed chicken thighs*
- *2 cups chopped smoked sausage*

- 2 cups chopped onion
- 2 cups chopped bell pepper
- 2 ribs celery
- 6 minced garlic cloves
- 2 tbsps. smoked paprika
- 2 tbsps. dried thyme
- Cayenne pepper
- 2 tbsps. Cajun spice blend
- 6 cups tomatoes with juice, divided
- ¼ tsp. hot pepper sauce
- 4 cups chicken broth
- 4 cups water
- Salt and pepper, to taste

Directions: In a large stockpot, warm the olive oil and lightly brown the first 6 ingredients. In a sizable bowl, mix paprika, seasonings, thyme, cayenne, and Cajun spice blend.
Sprinkle the vegetable and meat mixture with the spice mixture, then add tomatoes and hot sauce, and stir well to combine.
Ladle the ingredients into sanitized quart jars, filling them no more than halfway.
Meanwhile, place the broth, tomato juice, and water in the stockpot and bring it to a boil, deglazing the bottom of the pot.
Ladle 2 cups of hot liquid into each jar, allowing 1 inch of headspace.
You can top up with water if you need to.
Process the sealed jars in a pressure canner for 90 minutes at 10 PSI, adjusting for altitude.

Nutrition: Calories: 767.9; Fat: 35.8g; Carbs: 72.9g; Protein: 35.1g

88. Crumb Meatballs with Sauce

Preparation Time: 15 minutes
Servings: 1 quart
Cooking Time: 1 hour & 40 minutes

Ingredients:
- 5 lbs. ground meat
- 2 cups very fine crumbs
- 2 tbsps. salt
- 2 tbsps. dried parsley
- 1 tbsp. garlic powder
- 1 tbsp. onion powder
- ½ batch marinara spaghetti sauce

Directions: Combine the meat, breadcrumbs, salt, parsley flakes, garlic powder, and onion powder in a large bowl, using your hands to mix well. Form very firm meatballs.
Place 8 to 10 meatballs into each sanitized quart jar. Don't overfill the jars with meatballs because you want to leave room for the sauce.
Heat marinara sauce until it is simmering, about 10 minutes. Cover the meatballs with hot marinara sauce.
Very gently use a rubber spatula to remove any air pockets so that the sauce occupies the jar, leaving some headspace. Can for 90 minutes in a pressure canner at 10 PSI, adjusting for altitude.

Nutrition: Calories: 219.1; Fat: 8.5g; Carbs: 15.6g; Protein: 20.3g

89. Stewing Beef

Preparation Time: 15 minutes
Servings: 5 pints
Cooking Time: 1 hour & 40 minutes

Ingredients:
- 5 lbs. Stewing beef
- Water
- Pickling salt

Directions: Trim any gristle off the stewed beef, then cut it into strips or into cubes. Heat a skillet sprayed with cooking spray. Brown the stewed beef in batches and keep it in a covered bowl to keep it hot.
Pack the beef in sterilized jars leaving a 1-inch headspace. Add a ½ tablespoon of pickling salt in each jar. Add boiling water or stock, then remove the bubbles.
Transfer the sealed jars to the pressure canner and process them at 10 pounds for 75 minutes. Wait for the pressure canner to depressurize to zero before removing the jars.
Arrange the jars on a cooling rack for 24 hours then store in a cool dry place.

Nutrition: Calories: 185.9; Fat: 6.1g; Carbs: 0g; Protein 30.5g

90. Pressure Canned Fish

Preparation Time: 15 minutes
Servings: 10 pints
Cooking Time: 1 hour & 40 minutes

Ingredients:
- 20 11-inch blue backs
- Onions
- 2 tbsps. pickling salt
- 9 tbsps. white vinegar
- 9 tbsps. ketchup

Directions: In a sizable bowl, mix salt, vinegar, and ketchup. Now layer the ingredients in the sterilized jars so that you start with fish, onions, and a tablespoon of the vinegar mixture.
Repeat with all the jars, leaving a headspace of ¼ inch. Arrange the sealed jars in the pressure canner and process them at 11 lbs. for 100 minutes.
Wait for the pressure canner to depressurize to zero before removing the jars. Arrange the jars on a cooling rack for 24 hours then store in a cool dry place.
Nutrition: Calories: 137.7; Fat: 3.6g; Carbs: 0g; Protein 25.3g

91. Beef, Lamb, and Venison
Preparation Time: 15 minutes   **Cooking Time: 1 hour & 25 minutes**
Servings: 8 pints

Ingredients:
- 8 lbs. ground beef, lamb, or venison
- 4 tsps. salt, divided
- White vinegar

Directions: Prepare the jars by cleaning them well. Set a rack in a pressure canner then put 3 to 4 inches of water. Fill your jars with a couple inches of water so they do not float, then place them in the canner. Simmer until ready to fill the jars. Do not boil the water. Add water in a large pot and boil.
Cook the meat within 10 minutes, or until lightly browned in a large skillet set over medium-high heat. Drain off any fat.
Remove it from the canner, empty into the sink, and place on a cutting board on a nearby countertop.
Pack the meat into the prepared jars, leaving 1 inch of headspace. Add ½ teaspoon of salt per pint.
Ladle in the boiling water, leaving 1 inch of headspace. Release any air bubbles using a nonmetallic utensil.
Rinse the rim of the jar with a solution of diluted vinegar and water to remove any greasy film. Seal with the lid and ring. Repeat with the remaining jars, meat, and salt.
Arrange the jars on a rack in your pressure canner. Lock the lid in place, boil, and let the canner vent for 10 minutes. Place a weighted gauge or pressure regulator on the vent.
Process for 1 hour and 15 minutes at 11 pounds (454 g) on a dial gauge or at 10 pounds (4.5 kg) on a weighted gauge. Adjust your temperature to maintain an even pressure. Turn off the heat. Let the pressure drop to zero before opening the lid.
Remove the jars from your canner. Set aside to cool, undisturbed, for 12 hours.
Check the lids for proper seals. Remove the rings, wipe the jars, label and date them, and transfer to a cupboard or pantry. Refrigerate any jars that don't seal properly, and use within 3 days. Properly sealed jars will last in the cupboard for 12 months.
Nutrition: Calories: 29.8; Fat: 18.8g; Carbs: 0g; Protein: 19.2g

92. Buttered Chicken Breast
Preparation Time: 15 minutes   **Cooking Time: 1 hour & 30 minutes**
Servings: 8 pints

Ingredients:
- 18 medium boneless and skinless chicken breasts
- 1 ½ tbsps. of salt
- 4 ½ cups of water
- Butter or Olive Oil for frying in skillet

Directions: Cook each side of the chicken in a skillet with some butter or olive oil, about 8-10 minutes. Remove from the heat when the chicken is white and cooked all the way through. If you poke it with a fork, the juices should run clear.
In each pint jar, place a ½ teaspoon of salt and 2 chicken breasts. Fill the jar with water.
Can for 70 minutes at 10 pounds of pressure for the weighted gauge of the pressure canner or 11 pounds if the pressure canner has a dial gauge.
Remove the jars, and let cool until it is room temperature, which may take about a day.
Nutrition: Calories: 44.8; Fat: 0.9g; Carbs: 0g; Protein: 9.2g

93. Canned Whole Clams

Preparation Time: 15 minutes
Servings: 7 pints
Cooking Time: 1 hour & 10 minutes

Ingredients:
- *5 lbs. Clam*
- *3 tbsps. salt*
- *2 tbsps. lemon juice*

Directions: Keep the clams cold in ice until you are ready to pressure can them. Scrub the shells then stream them over water for 5 minutes. Open the clams and remove meat. Save the juices.
Add a gallon of water in a mixing bowl then add (at most) 3 tbsps. of salt. Wash the clam meat in the salted water.
Add water in a shallow saucepan, then add lemon juice. Bring the water to boil. Add the clam meat and boil for 2 minutes. Heat the reserved clam juices until boiling.
Drain the meat and pack it loosely into the jars leaving a 1-inch headspace. Pour the hot clam juice over the meat, then remove the bubbles. You may add boiling water if you run out of the clam juice.
Process the sealed and cleaned jars at 10 pounds of pressure for 60 minutes. Wait for the pressure canner to depressurize to zero before removing the jars.
Place the jars on a cooling rack for 12-24 hours undisturbed, and then store in a cool dry place.

Nutrition: Calories: 147.9; Fat: 1.8g; Carbs: 4.8g; Protein: 25.7g

94. Canned Shad Fish

Preparation Time: 15 minutes
Servings: 6
Cooking Time: 1 hour & 40 minutes

Ingredients:
- *Shad*
- *Salt*

Directions: Put the jars into simmering water (not boiling) until you are ready to use them. Prepare the pressure canner.
Make some brine by dissolving a cup of salt in a gallon of water. Cut the fish to pieces of jar length and allow them to soak in the brine for an hour. Afterwards, drain the pieces for 10 minutes.
To pack the pieces into the jars, make sure that the skin side is against the glass. Set the canner to 10 pounds of pressure and process for 1 hour and 40 minutes. Allow 24 hours for cooling and check the seals.

Nutrition: Calories: 362.3; Fat: 25.1g; Carbs: 0g; Protein: 31.4g

95. Chicken and Potato

Preparation Time: 15 minutes
Servings: 6 pints
Cooking Time: 1 hour & 30 minutes

Ingredients:
- *2 tbsps. butter*
- *4 cubed chicken breasts*
- *4 cubed chicken thighs*
- *1 chopped onion*
- *6 minced garlic cloves*
- *6 cups potatoes*
- *8 cups divided chicken broth*
- *½ cup ClearJel*
- *2 tbsps. distilled white vinegar*

Directions: In a sizable skillet, heat the butter over medium-high heat. Add the onion, chicken, and garlic, and cook for 10 minutes, stirring occasionally.
Arrange the hot jars on a cutting board. Evenly distribute the cooked chicken mixture among the jars.
Next, evenly distribute the potatoes among the jars, being sure to leave a generous 1-inch headspace.
In the same skillet, add 6 cups of chicken broth and bring to a boil over high heat.
In a small bowl, whisk the ClearJel with the remaining 2 cups of broth until well distributed. Add the mixture to the broth as you stir then boil for another minute.
Arrange the hot jars on a cutting board. Using a funnel, ladle the hot gravy into the jars, leaving a 1-inch headspace.
Remove any air bubbles and add additional gravy if necessary to maintain the 1-inch headspace. Rinse the rim of each jar with a warm washcloth dipped in distilled white vinegar and seal the lids.
Pour 3 quarts of water to the pressure canner and add 2 tablespoons distilled white vinegar. Arrange the jars in the pressure canner and bring to a boil over high heat while locked.
Vent the pressure canner for 10 minutes. Seal the vent and keep heating to reach 11 PSI for a dial gauge and 10 PSI for a weighted gauge. Can for 90 minutes (quarts) and 75 minutes (pints).

Nutrition: Calories: 296.1; Fat: 6.1g; Carbs: 34.4g; Protein: 23.7g

96. Canned Beef Cubes

Preparation Time: 15 minutes
Cooking Time: 1 hour & 40 minutes
Servings: 7

Ingredients:
- 5lbs beef stew meat
- 1 tbsp vegetable oil
- 12 cups cubed potatoes
- 8 cups sliced carrots
- 3 cups chopped celery
- 3 cups chopped onion
- 1 ½ tbsps. salt
- 1 tbsp. thyme
- ½ tbsp. pepper
- Water to cover

Directions: Brown meat in a large saucepot with some oil. Add the vegetables and all seasonings, then cover with water. Boil the stew and remove it from heat.
Scoop the hot stew into hot quart jars. Leave a 1-inch headspace. If needed, remove air bubbles to adjust the headspace, then rinse the rims of the jars with a paper towel, dampened and clean.
Now apply the 2-piece metal caps. Can the quart jars in a pressure canner for about 90 minutes at 11 pounds of pressure if using a dial-gauge canner (or 10 pounds of pressure if using a weighted-gauge canner).

Nutrition: Calories: 876.8; Fat: 22.4g; Carbs: 59.1g; Protein: 104.8g

97. Canned Chili Beans and Beef

Preparation Time: 15 minutes
Cooking Time: 2 hours & 10 minutes
Servings: 9

Ingredients:
- 3 cups pinto bean or red kidney beans
- 5 ½ cups water
- 5 tbsps. salt
- 3 lbs. ground beef
- 1½ cups onion, chopped
- 1 cup pepper, chopped
- 1 tbsp. black pepper
- 6 tbsps. chili powder
- 8 cups tomatoes

Directions: Place beans in a 2-qt. saucepan, then add cold water to 2-3 inches above the beans. Cover and leave for about 12-18 hours to soak. Drain the beans and discard water.
Place the beans in a saucepot with 5-½ cups water. Season with 2 tbsp of salt and bring to boil for about 25 minutes. Simmer for about 30 minutes. Meanwhile, brown beef with onions and pepper (optional) in a skillet, then drain the fat off.
Add 3 tablespoons salt and the remaining ingredients together with the cooked beans and simmer for about 5 minutes. Make sure not to thicken.
Scoop hot chili stew into hot pint jars. Leave a 1-inch headspace. Do not use quart jars. If needed, remove air bubbles and adjust headspace.
Rinse the rims of the jars using a clean, damp paper towel. Now apply the 2-piece metal caps.
Can the pint jars in a pressure canner for about 75 minutes at 11 pounds of pressure if using a dial-gauge canner (or 10 pounds of pressure if using a weighted-gauge canner).

Nutrition: Calories: 555.8; Fat: 11.2g; Carbs: 50.8g; Protein: 62.1g

98. Canned Chicken in a Jars

Preparation Time: 15 minutes
Cooking Time: 1 hour & 30 minutes
Servings: 2

Ingredients:
- 1 lb. chicken
- ½ tbsp. salt

Directions: Slice the chicken and place it into quart jars leaving a 1-inch headspace. Put salt into the jars then rinse the jar rims with a clean damp towel. Now apply the 2-piece metal caps.
Can the pint jars in a pressure canner for about 90 minutes at 11 pounds of pressure if using a dial-gauge canner or 10 pounds of pressure if using a weighted-gauge can.

Nutrition: Calories: 341.8; Fat: 6.7g; Carbs: 0g; Protein: 65.9g

99. Fish Chowder

Preparation Time: 15 minutes
Cooking Time: 1 hour & 40 minutes
Servings: 8

Ingredients:
- ¾ cup chopped onion
- 3 tbsps. butter
- ½ cup chopped celery
- 2 cups diced potatoes
- 1 tsp. garlic powder
- 2 cups chicken broth
- 2 diced carrots
- 1 tsp black pepper
- 1 tsp salt
- 32 oz. canned fish
- 1 tsp. dried dill weed
- 15 oz. canned creamed corn
- 12 oz. canned evaporated milk
- ½ lb. shredded cheddar cheese

Directions: In a pot over medium heat, melt butter. Cook celery, onion, and garlic powder for 5 minutes in the melted butter. Stir in carrots, potatoes, salt, broth, pepper, and dill.

Boil, then reduce the heat to low. Cover and simmer for 20 minutes. Stir in milk, cheese, corn, and fish. Cook until cheese melts.

Fill jars with fish chowder to 1/2 inch from the top. Put the jars in your canner then fill with water up to the jar rings.

Close and lock the pressure canner and bring to a boil over high heat, then add cooking weight to the top.

After 20 minutes, reduce the heat to medium and cook for 75 minutes. Turn off the heat then leave the canner alone until it has cooled completely to room temperature.

After canner has cooled, remove the jars from the canner and check for sealing. If the jars have sealed, store for up to 2 years; if not, use the fish chowder right away.

Nutrition: Calories: 248.8; Fat: 7.9g; Carbs: 14.3g; Protein: 26.7g

100. Fish Rice Casserole

Preparation Time: 15 minutes
Cooking Time: 1 hour & 10 minutes
Servings: 4

Ingredients:
- 14 oz. fish
- 2 cups cooked rice, divided
- 1 egg
- ¼ cup milk
- ¼ tsp. salt
- ¼ tsp. pepper
- 2 tbsps. butter

Directions: Grease an 8-inch baking dish. Preheat the oven to 375°F. Drain the fish, saving the juice to use later. Spread 1 cup of the rice in the baking dish.

Spread the fish over the rice, flaking it finely. Pour the reserved fish juice over the fish. Spread the remaining 1 cup of rice over the top. In a bowl, mix the milk, egg, salt, and pepper. Transfer the egg mixture evenly over the casserole. Dot with butter.

Bake until heated through and golden, about 30 minutes. Fill the jars with fish and rice casserole. Put the jars in canner and fill with water to the jar rings.

Close and lock pressure canner and bring to a boil over high heat, then add cooking weight to the top. After 20 minutes, turn heat to medium and cook for 75 minutes.

Turn off heat and leave canner alone until it has cooled completely to room temperature. After canner has cooled, remove jars from the canner and check for sealing.

Nutrition: Calories: 209.4; Fat: 4.8g; Carbs: 18.6g; Protein: 21.3g

101. Canned Oysters

Preparation Time: 15 minutes
Cooking Time: 1 hour & 10 minutes
Servings: 6

Ingredients:
- 5 lbs. oysters
- salt
- water

Directions: Wash the oysters in clean water, then heat them in an oven at 400°F for 7 minutes to open. Cool them in ice-cold water. Remove the meat, placing it in water containing salt.

Drain the meat and pack in the jars, leaving a 1-inch headspace. Add 1/2 tbsp. of salt in each half-pint jar and add water maintaining the headspace.

Wipe the jar rims, then place the lids and the rings. Can for 75 minutes at 10 pounds. Wait for the pressure canner to depressurize to zero before removing the jars from the canner.

Place the jars on a cooling rack, then store in a cool dry place.

Nutrition: Calories: 67.9; Fat: 2.7g; Carbs: 0g; Protein 7.2g

102. Canned Trout

Preparation Time: 15 minutes **Cooking Time: 1 hour & 45 minutes**
Servings: 8

Ingredients:
- 6 whole trout
- 6 tbsps. lemon juice (1 tbsp. per jar)
- 6 rosemary springs

Directions: Place 1 rosemary spring in trout's cavity. Salt the inside with ½ tsp. of salt and close it. Pack jars with trout. Add 1 tbsp. of lemon juice to each jar.

Process for 1 hour and 45 minutes at 10 pounds of pressure for the weighted gauge of the pressure canner or 11 pounds if the pressure canner has a dial-gauge. Remove the jars and let cool until at room temperature.

Nutrition: Calories: 109.8; Fat: 5.8g; Carbs: 0g; Protein: 14.2g

103. Minced Clams

Preparation Time: 15 minutes **Cooking Time: 1 hour & 5 minutes**
Servings: 8

Ingredients:
- 2 lbs. live clams
- 1 tsp. salt in each jar
- boiling water
- citric acid

Directions: Scrub the clamshells thoroughly before rinsing and steaming for 5 minutes. Open to remove the meat; reserve the juices. Wash the collected clam meat with a mixture of water and salt (1 tsp per quart). Rinse and place in a pot filled with boiling water (1 gallon) and lemon juice (2 tbsps.) or citric acid (1/2 tsp).

Heat until boiling, and then boil for two minutes. Drain before placing in clean and hot Mason jars.

Pack the clam meat loosely before adding in the hot clam juice, filling the jars up to one inch from the top. After getting rid of air bubbles, adjust the jar lids. Process in the pressure canner for 1 hour (for pint jars) or 1 hour and 10 minutes (for quart jars).

Nutrition: Calories: 103.8; Fat: 3.7g; Carbs: 16.1g; Protein: 1.5g

104. Canned Mackerel

Preparation Time: 15 minutes **Cooking Time: 1 hour & 40 minutes**
Servings: 3

Ingredients:
- 2 lbs. mackerel fish
- vinegar
- salt

Directions: Rinse the fish in cold water mixed with vinegar (2 tbsps. for each quart). Discard the scales, head, fins, and tail of the fish, then wash thoroughly to remove all blood. Split the fish into lengthwise halves before cutting into 3 ½-inch long pieces. Put in clean and hot Mason jars, each filled with one tsp. of salt but without adding any liquid.

Adjust the lids on the jars before placing in the pressure canner. Process for one hour and forty minutes.

Nutrition: Calories: 103.9; Fat: 3.8g; Carbs: 16.1g; Protein: 1.4g

105. Canned Salmon

Preparation Time: 15 minutes **Cooking Time: 1 hour & 40 minutes**
Servings: 6

Ingredients:
- 5 lbs. salmon
- salt

Directions: Eviscerate the salmon immediately after catching it then clean it thoroughly with clean water. Chill it until you are ready to pressure can it. Remove the tail, the head, and the fins. Split the fish lengthwise then cut into small pieces that perfectly fit into your jars.

Pack the fish in sterilized jars leaving a 1-inch headspace. Add a tbsp. of salt in each jar if you desire. Rinse the jar rims with a damp paper towel then place the lids and the rings on the jar.

Pressure-can the jars in the pressure canner at 11 pounds pressure for 100 minutes. Wait for the pressure canner to depressurize to zero before removing the jars.

Transfer the jars on a cooling rack for 24 hours then store in a cool dry place.
Nutrition: Calories: 120.8; Fat: 5.1g; Carbs: 0g; Protein: 17.2g

CHAPTER 4: BEANS AND LEGUMES

106. White Beans

Preparation Time: 10 minutes
Cooking Time: 35 minutes
Servings: 28

Ingredients:
- 3¼ pounds dried white beans, soaked for 18 hours and drained
- 4½ tsps salt

Directions: In a Dutch oven, add beans and enough water to cover over high heat and cook until boiling. Adjust the heat to low then cook for about 30 minutes.
Drain the beans, reserving cooking liquid. In 7 (1-pint) hot sterilized jars, divide the beans and sprinkle with salt. Fill each jar with hot cooking liquid, leaving 1-inch space from the top. Run your knife around the insides of each jar to remove any air bubbles.
Clean any trace of food off the rims of jars with a clean, moist kitchen towel. Close each jar with a lid and screw on the ring.
Carefully place the jars in the pressure canner and process at 10 pounds pressure for about 75 minutes.
Remove the jars from pressure canner and place onto a wood surface several inches apart to cool completely.
After cooling with your finger, press the top of each jar's lid to ensure that the seal is tight. Store these canning jars in a cool, dark place.

Nutrition: Calories: 139.8; Fat: 0.4g; Carbs: 3.1g; Protein: 11.8g

107. Chickpeas

Preparation Time: 10 minutes
Servings: 8
Cooking Time: 35 minutes

Ingredients:
- *1-pound dried chickpeas, soaked for 18 hours and drained*
- *1 tsp salt*

Directions: In a Dutch oven, add chickpeas and enough water to cover over high heat and cook until boiling. Adjust the heat to low then cook for about 30 minutes.
Drain the chickpeas, reserving cooking liquid. In 2 (1-pint) hot sterilized jars, divide the chickpeas and sprinkle with salt.
Fill each jar with hot cooking liquid, leaving 1-inch space from the top. Run your knife around the insides of each jar to remove any air bubbles.
Clean any trace of food off the rims of jars with a clean, moist kitchen towel. Close each jar with a lid and screw on the ring.
Carefully place the jars in the pressure canner and process at 10 pounds pressure for about 90 minutes.
Remove the jars from pressure canner and place onto a wood surface several inches apart to cool completely.
After cooling with your finger, press the top of each jar's lid to ensure that the seal is tight. Store these canning jars in a cool, dark place.

Nutrition: Calories: 177.9; Fat: 3.1g; Carbs: 33.7g; Protein: 11.4g

108. Pinto Beans Chili

Preparation Time: 15 minutes
Servings: 18
Cooking Time: 40 minutes

Ingredients:
- *2 pounds dry pinto beans, rinsed and drained*
- *3–4 bay leaves*
- *Salt, as needed*
- *1 tbsp olive oil*
- *2 onions, chopped*
- *2 (28-ounce) cans petite diced tomatoes*
- *1 (15-ounce) can tomato sauce*
- *2 cups beef broth*
- *3 tbsps chili powder*
- *2 tbsps ground cumin*
- *2 tsps garlic powder*
- *1 tsps dried oregano*
- *1 tsps dried thyme*
- *Ground black pepper, as needed*

Directions: In a large stockpot of water, add beans, bay leaves, 1 tablespoon of salt over high heat and cook until boiling. Reduce the heat to low and cook for about 30–35 minutes.
Meanwhile, heat oil in a frying pan over medium heat and sauté the onion for about 4–5 minutes. Drain the beans and return to the same pot.
In the pot of beans, add the cooked onion and remaining ingredients and stir to combine. Put the pan over high heat and bring to a boil.
In 9 (1-pint) hot sterilized jars, divide the chili, leaving 1-inch space from the top. Run your knife around the insides of each jar to remove any air bubbles.
Clean any trace of food off the rims of jars with a clean, moist kitchen towel. Close each jar with a lid and screw on the ring.
Carefully place the jars in the pressure canner and process at 10 pounds pressure for about 90 minutes.
Remove the jars from pressure canner and place onto a wood surface several inches apart to cool completely.
After cooling with your finger, press the top of each jar's lid to ensure that the seal is tight. Store these canning jars in a cool, dark place.

Nutrition: Calories: 219.9; Fat: 1.8g; Carbs: 38.3g; Protein: 13.1g

109. Kidney Beans Chili

Preparation Time: 15 minutes
Servings: 18
Cooking Time: 40 minutes

Ingredients:
- *3 cups dried red kidney beans, soaked overnight and drained*
- *1 tbsp salt*
- *2 cups onion, chopped*
- *1 cup sweet bell pepper, seeded & chopped*
- *6 garlic cloves, minced*
- *¼ cup fresh parsley, minced*
- *8 cups tomato juice*
- *½ cup tomato paste*
- *3 tbsps red chili powder*
- *1 tsp ground black pepper*
- *2 tsps dried thyme*
- *2 tsps ground cumin*

Directions: In a Dutch oven, add beans and enough water to cover over high heat and cook until boiling. Reduce the heat to low and cook for about 30 minutes. Drain the beans well.
For sauce: In a saucepan, add remaining ingredients over medium heat and cook until boiling. Stir in the cooked beans and cook until boiling.
In 9 (1-pint) hot sterilized jars, divide the beans. Fill each jar with hot sauce mixture, leaving 1-inch space from the top.
Run your knife around the insides of each jar to remove any air bubbles. Wipe any trace of food off the rims of jars with a clean, moist kitchen towel.
Close each jar with a lid and screw on the ring. Carefully place the jars in the pressure canner and process at 10 pounds pressure for about 75 minutes.
Remove the jars from pressure canner and place onto a wood surface several inches apart to cool completely. After cooling with your finger, press the top of each jar's lid to ensure that the seal is tight. Store these canning jars in a cool, dark place.

Nutrition: Calories: 137.9; Fat: 0.4g; Carbs: 26.8g; Protein: 8.4g

110. White Beans and Corn Chili
Preparation Time: 15 minutes
Cooking Time: 40 minutes
Servings: 14

Ingredients:
- 1-pound white beans, soaked for 6 hours and drained
- 6 cups chicken broth
- 1-pound frozen corn
- 1 medium onion, chopped
- 7 ounces canned green chilies
- 6 garlic cloves
- 4 tsps ground cumin
- 1 tsp dried oregano
- 2 tsps cayenne pepper

Directions: In a Dutch oven, add beans and enough water to cover over high heat and cook until boiling. Adjust the heat to low and cook for about 30 minutes. Drain the beans completely and set aside.
In 7 (1-pint) hot sterilized jars, divide the beans. Fill each jar with hot broth mixture, leaving 1-inch space from the top.
Run your knife around the insides of each jar to remove any air bubbles. Clean any trace of food off the rims of jars with a clean, moist kitchen towel.
Close each jar with a lid and screw on the ring. Carefully place the jars in the pressure canner and process at 10 pounds pressure for about 75 minutes.
Remove the jars from pressure canner and place onto a wood surface several inches apart to cool completely. After cooling with your finger, press the top of each jar's lid to ensure that the seal is tight. Store these canning jars in a cool, dark place.

Nutrition: Calories: 165.8; Fat: 1.9g; Carbs: 28.1g; Protein: 11.6g

111. Black-Eyed Peas
Preparation Time: 10 minutes
Cooking Time: 30 minutes
Servings: 12

Ingredients:
- 1½ pounds dried black-eyed peas, soaked overnight and drained
- 6 tbps onions, chopped
- 4 tsps dried thyme
- 1½ tsp kosher salt
- 30 peppercorns

Directions: In a Dutch oven, add black-eyed peas and enough water to cover over high heat and cook until boiling. Adjust the heat to low and cook for about 30 minutes.
Drain the black-eyed peas, reserving cooking liquid. In 3 (1-pint) hot sterilized jars, divide the black-eyed peas, onion, thyme, salt, and peppercorn.
Fill each jar with hot cooking liquid, leaving 1-inch space from the top. Run your knife around the insides of each jar to remove any air bubbles.
Clean any trace of food off the rims of jars with a clean, moist kitchen towel. Close each jar with a lid and screw on the ring.
Carefully place the jars in the pressure canner and process at 10 pounds pressure for about 75 minutes.
Remove the jars from pressure canner and place onto a wood surface several inches apart to cool completely. After cooling with your finger, press the top of each jar's lid to ensure that the seal is tight. Store these canning jars in a cool, dark place.

Nutrition: Calories: 195.8; Fat: 0.7g; Carbs: 33.7g; Protein: 13.7g

112. Red Lentils

Preparation Time: 10 minutes
Cooking Time: 10 minutes
Servings: 8

Ingredients:
- 2 cups red lentils, rinsed
- 4 cups chicken broth
- 2 small brown onions, chopped finely

Directions: In a Dutch oven, add lentils, onion, and broth over high heat and cook until boiling. Now set the heat to low and cook for about 5 minutes.
In 4 (1-pint) hot sterilized jars, divide the lentils. Fill each jar with hot cooking liquid, leaving 1-inch space from the top.
Run your knife around the insides of each jar to remove any air bubbles. Clean any trace of food off the rims of jars with a clean, moist kitchen towel.
Close each jar with a lid and screw on the ring. Carefully place the jars in the pressure canner and process at 10 pounds pressure for about 75 minutes.
Remove the jars from pressure canner and place onto a wood surface several inches apart to cool completely.
After cooling with your finger, press the top of each jar's lid to ensure that the seal is tight. Store these canning jars in a cool, dark place.

Nutrition: Calories: 195.8; Fat: 1.1g; Carbs: 30.7g; Protein: 15.2g

113. Corn

Preparation Time: 15 minutes
Cooking Time: 55 minutes
Servings: 12

Ingredients:
- 12 ears corn
- 1½ tsp salt

Directions: Husk corn and remove silk. Wash corn cobs and cut corn from cob. In 3 (1-pint) hot sterilized jars, divide the corn and salt.
Fill each jar with hot water, leaving 1-inch space from the top. Run your knife around the insides of each jar to remove any air bubbles.
Clean any trace of food off the rims of jars with a clean, moist kitchen towel. Close each jar with a lid and screw on the ring.
Carefully place the jars in the pressure canner and process at 10 pounds pressure for about 55 minutes.
Remove the jars from pressure canner and place onto a wood surface several inches apart to cool completely.
After cooling with your finger, press the top of each jar's lid to ensure that the seal is tight. Store these canning jars in a cool, dark place.

Nutrition: Calories: 131.8; Fat: 1.7g; Carbs: 28.9g; Protein: 5.2g

114. Sweet and Sour Beans

Preparation Time: 15 minutes
Cooking Time: 30 minutes
Servings: 8

Ingredients:
- 1 pound navy beans
- ½ cup leeks, chopped
- 2 cups water
- 2 cups ketchup
- 1 cup maple syrup
- ½ cup molasses
- 2 tbps brown sugar
- 1½ tsp mustard powder
- Salt and ground black pepper, as needed
- ½ cup white vinegar

Directions: In a Dutch oven, add beans and enough water to cover over high heat and cook until boiling. Remove the pan of beans from heat and set aside, covered for about 30–45 minutes.
Drain the beans and then add enough fresh water to cover. Add the leeks and cook for about 15–20 minutes. Remove the pan of beans from heat and drain water.
In a nonreactive saucepan, add 2 cups of water and remaining ingredients (except for vinegar) and bring to a gentle boil, stirring continuously.
Remove the pan of cooking mixture from heat and stir in vinegar. In 4 (1-pint) hot sterilized jars, divide the beans. Fill each jar with hot vinegar mixture, leaving 1-inch space from the top.
Run your knife around the insides of each jar to remove any air bubbles. Clean any trace of food off the rims of jars with a clean, moist kitchen towel.

Close each jar with a lid and screw on the ring. Carefully place the jars in the pressure canner and process at 10 pounds pressure for about 75 minutes.

Remove the jars from pressure canner and place onto a wood surface several inches apart to cool completely. After cooling with your finger, press the top of each jar's lid to ensure that the seal is tight. Store these canning jars in a cool, dark place.

Nutrition: Calories: 388.8; Fat: 0.9g; Carbs: 84.8g; Protein: 13.9g

115. Baked Beans

Preparation Time: 15 minutes
Servings: 6

Cooking Time: 12 minutes

Ingredients:
- *1-pound dried navy beans*
- *2 bay leaves*
- *1 cup onion, chopped finely*
- *6 tbsps tomato paste*
- *3 tbsps brown sugar*
- *1½ tbsp Worcestershire sauce*
- *1½ tsp mustard powder*
- *1½ tsp salt*
- *1½ tsp ground black pepper*

Directions: In a Dutch oven, add beans and enough water to cover over high heat and cook until boiling. Remove the pan of beans from heat and set aside, covered for about 1 hour.

Drain the beans and then add enough fresh water to cover. In the pan of beans, add bay leaves over high heat and cook until boiling. Boil for about 2 minutes. Drain the beans, reserving the cooking liquid.

For sauce: In a large microwave-safe bowl, add remaining ingredients and stir to combine. Add reserved 3 cups of hot cooking liquid and microwave or about 5 minutes.

Remove the bowl of sauce from the microwave and mix well. In 3 (1-pint) hot sterilized jars, divide the beans. Fill each jar with hot sauce mixture, leaving 1-inch space from the top.

Run your knife around the insides of each jar to remove any air bubbles. Clean any trace of food off the rims of jars with a clean, moist kitchen towel.

Close each jar with a lid and screw on the ring. Carefully place the jars in the pressure canner and process at 10 pounds pressure for about 75 minutes.

Remove the jars from pressure canner and place onto a wood surface several inches apart to cool completely. After cooling with your finger, press the top of each jar's lid to ensure that the seal is tight. Store these canning jars in a cool, dark place.

Nutrition: Calories: 299.8; Fat: 0.9g; Carbs: 56.5g; Protein: 18.3g

CHAPTER 5: SOUPS, STEW, SAUCES, AND BROTH

116. Beef & Potato Stew

Preparation Time: 15 minutes
Canning Time: 1 ¼ hour
Cooking Time: 15 minutes
Servings: 12

Ingredients:
- 1 tablespoon canola oil
- 1 ½ pound beef stew meat, cubed
- 4 cups beef broth
- 1 cup onion, chopped
- 3 carrots, peeled and sliced
- 1 cup celery, sliced
- 2 large potatoes, peeled and cubed
- 1 (28-ounce) can diced tomatoes with juice
- 1 tablespoon sugar
- 2 teaspoons salt
- ½ teaspoon ground black pepper
- 1 ½ teaspoon Italian seasoning
- 1 cup frozen peas

Directions: In a Dutch oven, heat the canola oil over medium-high heat and sear the beef cubes for about 4–5 minutes. Add in the remaining ingredients and cook for about 10 minutes.
In 6 (1-pint) hot sterilized jars, divide the soup leaving about ½-inch space from the top.
Slide a small knife around the insides of each jar to remove air bubbles.
Clean any trace of food off the rims of jars with a clean, moist kitchen towel.
Carefully place the jars in the pressure canner and process at 10 pounds pressure for about 75 minutes.
Remove the jars from the pressure canner and place them onto a wood surface several inches apart to cool completely. After cooling with your finger, press the top of each jar's lid to ensure that the seal is tight.
Store these canning jars in a cool, dark place.

Nutrition: Calories: 209.9; Fat: 5.4g; Carbs: 18.1g; Fiber: 3.5g; Sugar: 5.5g; Protein: 21.6g

117. Beef Broth

Preparation Time: 20 minutes
Canning Time: 20 minutes
Cooking Time: 7 hours and 5 minutes
Servings: 20

Ingredients:
- 4 pounds meaty beef soup bones
- 3 celery ribs, cut into chunks
- 3 medium carrots, peeled and chopped roughly
- 2 medium onions, quartered
- ½ cup warm water
- 3 bay leaves
- 3 garlic cloves
- 8–10 whole peppercorns
- 3–4 sprigs of fresh parsley
- 1 teaspoon dried thyme
- 1 teaspoon dried oregano
- 1 teaspoon dried marjoram
- Cold water, as needed

Directions: Preheat your oven to 450°F. In a large roasting pan, place the beef bones.
Roast for approximately 30 minutes. After 30 minutes of roasting, place the carrots, celery, and onions into the roasting pan with bones. Roast for approximately 30 minutes.
Remove the roasting pan of bones and vegetables from the oven and drain off the grease.
In a stockpot, place the roasted beef bones and vegetables.
In the roasting pan, add warm water and with a spoon, scrape up the browned bits from the bottom.
In the stockpot, add the roasting pan juices, bay leaves, and garlic, peppercorns, parsley, and dried herbs.
Add enough water to cover the mixture. Place the pan over high heat and cook until boiling.
Now set the heat to low and cook, covered, for about 2 hours. Uncover the pot and simmer, covered, for about 4 hours. Through a strainer, strain the broth, discarding the solids.
In 5 (1-pint) hot sterilized jars, divide the broth, leaving about ½-inch space from the top.
Slide a small knife around the insides of each jar to remove air bubbles.
Clean any trace of food off the rims of jars with a clean, moist kitchen towel.
Carefully place the jars in the pressure canner and process at 10 pounds pressure for about 20 minutes.
Remove the jars from the pressure canner and place them onto a wood surface several inches apart to cool completely. After cooling with your finger, press the top of each jar's lid to ensure that the seal is tight.
Store these canning jars in a cool, dark place.

Nutrition: Calories: 114.8; Fat: 2.9g; Carbs: 4.3g; Fiber: 0.4g; Sugar: 0.8g; Protein: 16.7g

118. Mexican Beef and Sweet Potato Soup

Preparation Time: 90 minutes
Canning Time: 75 minutes
Cooking Time: 20 minutes
Servings: 8

Ingredients:

- 1 tablespoon vegetable oil
- 2-1/2 quarts beef broth
- 2-1/pounds beef chuck roast, trimmed of fat and slice into one-inch dices
- 4 Roma tomatoes, seeded and sliced
- 1 medium sweet potato, peeled and sliced
- 8 1-inch diameter carrots, peeled and cut into 1/4-inch rounds
- 1 cup frozen or fresh whole kernel corn
- 1 large onion, sliced
- 2 jalapeño peppers, stemmed, seeded, and thinly sliced
- 2 poblano peppers, stemmed, seeded, and sliced
- 1 tablespoon salt
- 6 garlic cloves, minced
- ½ tablespoon ground black pepper
- ½ tablespoon chili powder

Directions: Pour 1/2 tablespoon of vegetable oil in a 6-quart pot and place over low-medium heat. Add half of the beef cubes. Fry and stir to turn brown. Move the beef into a small bowl. Do the same with the remaining 1/2 tablespoon of oil and the beef. Transfer all the meat to the pot and add the broth. Reduce the heat and allow it to boil. Simmer covered until the beef is soft.

Add sweet potatoes, carrots, tomatoes, onions, corn, garlic, jalapeno peppers, poblano peppers, salt, black pepper, and chili powder to the beef mixture in the pot. Cover and leave it to boil for 5 minutes.

Ladle vegetables and beef into the canning jars by filling each halfway. Pour hot broth into every jar and leave one-inch headspace. Remove air bubbles, wipe the jar rims, adjust the lids, and screw the band.

Put the filled jars in a pressure canner at 11 pounds pressure for dial-gauge or 10 pounds for the weighted-gauge canner. Process heat jars for 75 minutes, adjusting for altitude then, turn off the heat and let pressure drop naturally so, remove the lid and cool the jars in the canner for 5 minutes. Take out the jars and cool. Inspect lids seal after 24 hours.

Nutrition: Calories: 376.8; Fat: 5.9g; Carbs: 6.1g; Protein: 3.1g

119. Veggie Stew

Preparation Time: 15 minutes
Canning Time: 55 minutes
Cooking Time: 10 minutes
Servings: 14

Ingredients:

- 4 pounds tomatoes, cored and chopped
- 2 cups lima beans
- 2 cups uncooked corn kernels
- 6 medium potatoes, peeled and cubed
- 12 medium carrots, peeled and sliced
- 1 cup celery stalk, sliced
- 2 medium onions, chopped
- Salt and ground black pepper, as needed
- 3 cups water

Directions: In a stockpot, add all ingredients over medium-high heat and cook until boiling.

Now set the heat to low and cook, uncovered for about 4–5 minutes.

In 7 (1-pint) hot sterilized jars, divide the stew, leaving about ½-inch space from the top.

Slide a small knife around the insides of each jar to remove air bubbles.

Clean any trace of food off the rims of jars with a clean, moist kitchen towel.

Carefully place the jars in the pressure canner and process at 10 pounds pressure for about 55 minutes.

Remove the jars from the pressure canner and place them onto a wood surface several inches apart to cool completely.

After cooling with your finger, press the top of each jar's lid to ensure that the seal is tight.

Store these canning jars in a cool, dark place.

Nutrition: Calories: 158.7; Fat: 0.7g; Carbs: 34.5g; Fiber: 7.1g; Sugar: 8.6g; Protein: 5.8g

120. Chicken Broth

Preparation Time: 20 minutes
Canning Time: 20 minutes
Cooking Time: 6 hours and 50 minutes
Servings: 32

Ingredients:

- 4 pounds tomatoes, cored and chopped
- 2 cups lima beans
- 2 cups uncooked corn kernels
- 6 medium potatoes, peeled and cubed
- 12 medium carrots, peeled and sliced
- 1 cup celery stalk, sliced
- 2 medium onions, chopped
- Salt and ground black pepper, as needed

- *3 cups water*

Directions: Preheat your oven to 425°F.
In a large roasting pan, place the chicken bones and spread the onions, carrots, celery, and garlic on top.
Roast for approximately 45 minutes, flipping once halfway through.
Remove the roasting pan from the oven and drain off the grease.
Transfer roasted beef bones and vegetables into a stockpot.
In the roasting pan, add 1 cup of water and scrape the browned bits from the bottom with a spoon.
In the stockpot, add the roasting pan juices and remaining ingredients except for water.
Add enough water to cover the mixture. Place the pan over high heat and cook until boiling.
Now set the heat to low and cook, uncovered, for about 4–6 hours.
Through a strainer, strain the broth.
In 8 (1-pint) hot sterilized jars, divide the broth, leaving about ½-inch space from the top.
Slide a small knife around the insides of each jar to remove air bubbles.
Clean any trace of food off the rims of jars with a clean, moist kitchen towel.
Carefully place the jars in the pressure canner and process at 10 pounds pressure for about 20 minutes.
Remove the jars from the pressure canner and place them onto a wood surface several inches apart to cool completely. After cooling with your finger, press the top of each jar's lid to ensure that the seal is tight.
Store these canning jars in a cool, dark place.

Nutrition: Calories: 112.8; Fat: 2.1g; Carbs: 1.2g; Fiber: 0.3g; Sugar: 0.5g; Protein: 20.8g

121. Asparagus Soup

Preparation Time: 15 minutes
Servings: 4 pints
Cooking Time: 1 hour & 25 minutes

Ingredients:
- 3 lbs. asparagus, fresh, cut stems
- 8 cups chicken broth/stock
- 1 cup shallots, minced
- 1 tbsp garlic, minced
- ½ tsp salt
- ¼ tsp white pepper, ground
- 2 tbsp olive oil

Directions: In a frying pan, add olive oil and sauté garlic and shallots until translucent. In a Stainless-steel saucepan, add broth and heat on medium flame. Remove from flame.
In hot jars, add asparagus to ¾ full, ¼ cup shallots/garlic, equal part of the pepper, and salt in each jar. Add stock. Leave headspace of 1-inch.
Transfer the hot soup into a hot jar with a ladle. Leave ¼ inch space on the top. Remove air bubbles. Clean the rim of the glass jar. Place the lid and apply a band around it. Adjust to ensure that the lid is tight.
Leave the pressure canner and vent steam for about 10 minutes. Close the vent and process for 75 minutes.
Turn off the canner, remove the lid after two minutes when pressure turns zero. Keep the jars in the canner for 5 minutes more.
Remove the jars and leave overnight. Reprocess if the jars are not sealed. Store in the refrigerator.

Nutrition: Calories: 103.8; Carbs: 6.9g; Fat: 5.7g; Protein: 1.2g

122. Potato and Leek Soup

Preparation Time: 30 minutes
Canning Time: 60 minutes
Cooking Time: 15 minutes
Servings: 7 quarts or 14 pints

Ingredients:
- 6 potatoes, peeled and cubed
- 4 cups stock, chicken or beef
- 5 pounds leeks, washed and cut into ¼-inch slices

Directions: Layer leaks at the bottom of each jar. Place a layer of potatoes on top of the leeks, followed by another layer of the sliced leeks.
Boil the chicken or beef stock before pouring it into the jars. Attach the lids to the jars and process in a pressure canner using 11 pounds for 60 minutes.

Nutrition: Carbs: 100.8g; Fat: 2.2g; Protein: 14.4g; Calories: 461.9

123. Veggie Soup

Preparation Time: 60 minutes
Canning Time: 60 minutes
Cooking Time: 15 minutes
Servings: 9-pint jars

Ingredients:
- 6 cups tomatoes (cored, peeled, chopped)
- 2 cups tomatillos (chopped)
- 1 cup onion (chopped)
- 1 cup carrots (chopped)
- 1 cup green bell pepper (chopped)
- 1 cup red bell pepper (chopped)
- 6 cups corn kernels
- ½ cup hot pepper (seeded, chopped)
- 1 teaspoon cayenne pepper
- 5 cups tomato juice
- 1 tablespoon hot sauce
- 2 teaspoons chili powder
- 2 teaspoons cumin (ground)
- 1 teaspoon salt
- 2 cups water
- 1 teaspoon black pepper

Directions: Sterilize the jars. Mix all the ingredients in a pot and bring to a boil.
Simmer uncovered for 15 minutes on low flame.
Distribute the solids and liquid among the jars, leaving 1 inch of headspace.
Remove air bubbles and clean the rims.
Cover the jars with the lid and secure the bands.
Process the jars for 60 minutes at 10 pounds pressure in a pressure canner.
Remove; allow cooling, and then label the jars.

Nutrition: Calories: 184.7; Fat: 1.7g; Carbs: 42.6g; Proteins: 7.1g

124. Fennel and Carrot Soup

Preparation Time: 35 minutes
Canning Time: 35 minutes
Cooking Time: 30 minutes
Servings: 9-pint jars

Ingredients:
- 1-pound fennel bulbs (trimmed)
- 1 tablespoon olive oil
- 4 ½ pounds carrots (peeled, sliced)
- 12 cups vegetable stock
- 2 teaspoons onion powder
- 2 tablespoons salt
- 1 teaspoon dried ginger (ground)
- 1 teaspoon dried thyme
- ½ teaspoon cumin (ground)
- 3 tablespoons lemon juice
- 1 teaspoon black pepper (ground)
- 1 teaspoon dried coriander (ground)

Directions: Sterilize the jars. Heat oil in a pot and sauté the fennel in it till translucent.
Mix in the carrots and 4 cups of vegetable broth and simmer for 30 minutes.
Leave to cool, and then puree the mixture. Return to the pot and mix in the rest of the ingredients.
Broil to boil and simmer for 20–30 minutes.
Ladle the mix immediately into the sterilized jars, leaving 1 inch of headspace.
Remove air bubbles and clean the rims.
Cover the jars with the lid and apply the bands ensuring that they are tightened. Process the jars for 35 minutes at 10 pounds pressure in a pressure canner. Remove; allow cooling, and then label the jars.

Nutrition: Calories: 47.9; Fat: 0.6g; Carbs: 9.8g; Proteins: 2.9g

125. Chicken Soup

Preparation Time: 15 minutes
Canning Time: 90 minutes
Cooking Time: 30 minutes
Servings: 8 pints

Ingredients:
- 16 cups chicken stock
- 3 cups cooked chicken, diced
- 1 ½ cups celery, diced
- 1 ½ cups carrots, sliced
- 1 cup onion, diced
- Salt to taste
- Pepper to taste
- 3 chicken bouillon cubes

Directions: Combine the chicken stock, chicken, celery, carrots, and onion in a large pot.
Bring the mixture to a boil. Lower the heat and simmer for 30 minutes.
Add the bouillon cubes and cook until the bouillon cubes are dissolved. Season the mixture with salt and pepper to taste. Pour the soup into sterile jars, leaving 1-inch headspace.
Wipe the jar rims clean and adjust the lids.
Process the filled jars in a pressure canner for 90 minutes at 10 pounds of pressure for a pressure canner with a weighted gauge (or 11 pounds if the pressure canner has a dial gauge).

Nutrition: Calories: 206.8; Fat: 7.9g; Fiber: 1.7g; Carbs: 7.9g; Protein: 6.2g

126. Beef Stew with Vegetables

Preparation Time: 15 minutes
Canning Time: 75 minutes
Cooking Time: 15 minutes
Servings: 6 pints

Ingredients:

- 5 pounds stewing beef, cut into 1 ½-inch cube
- 1 tablespoon vegetable oil
- 12 cups potatoes, peeled and cubed
- 3 cups celery, chopped
- 8 cups carrots, peeled and sliced
- 3 cups onions, chopped
- 4 ½ teaspoons salt
- 1 teaspoon dried thyme
- ½ teaspoon freshly ground black pepper
- Boiling water

Directions: In a large non-stick skillet, heat the oil and brown the beef.
Place the browned beef in a large saucepan and add the potatoes, celery, onions, carrots, pepper, salt, thyme, and boiling water to cover the ingredients. Simmer, stirring frequently, for 15 minutes.
Pour the stew into sterile jars, leaving 1-inch headspace. Clean the rims clean and adjust the lids.
Process in a pressure canner for 75 minutes at 10 pounds for a pressure canner with a weighted gauge (or 11 pounds if the pressure canner has a dial gauge).

Nutrition: Calories: 206.8; Fat: 7.9g; Fiber: 1.8g; Carbs: 7.8g; Protein: 6.3g

127. Five-Bean Medley

Preparation Time: 15 minutes
Canning Time: 90 minutes
Cooking Time: 10 minutes
Servings: 6 pints

Ingredients:

- 12 cups hot water
- 3 cups dried pinto beans (16 ounces)
- 2-1/2 cups dried kidney beans (16 ounces)
- 2-1/4 cups dried black beans (16 ounces)
- 2-1/4 cups dried split peas (16 ounces)
- 2-1/2 cups dried great northern beans (16 ounces)
- 7 teaspoons coarse sea salt (optional)

Directions: Add the water to the stockpot and bring to a boil on high heat.
Thoroughly rinse and clean the dried beans split peas, discarding any disfigured or shriveled beans and any rocks or debris.
If using, add 1 teaspoon of salt per quart jar or ½ teaspoon of salt per pint jar before filling with dried beans.
Using a ladle and funnel, fill each quart jar with 1 ½ cups of clean dried beans, split peas and each pint jar with ¾ cup. Pour the hot water over the beans, leaving 1 inch of headspace. Use an air bubble remover to remove the air and adjust the headspace with morel water to maintain the 1 inch of headspace.
Dip a warm washcloth in distilled white vinegar and wipe the rims of the jars. Set a lid and jar on each and tighten.
Set the jars in the pressure canner, place the lid, and allow it to boil while on high heat. You can vent for approximately 10 minutes. Lock the vent and heat further to attain a dial gauge of 11 PSI and a weighted gauge of 10 PSI. Process quart jars for 90 minutes and pint jars for around 75 minutes.

Nutrition: Calories: 119.2; Fat: 0.9g; Carbs: 21.9g; Protein: 8.2g

128. Vegetable Soup

Preparation Time: 15 minutes
Canning Time: 55 minutes
Cooking Time: 10 minutes
Servings: 7 quarts

Ingredients:

- 8 cups tomatoes, peeled, cored, and chopped
- 4 cups green lima beans
- 6 cups carrots, in ¾" slices
- 2 cups onions, chopped
- 6 cups potatoes, peeled and cubed
- 4 cups uncooked corn kernels
- 2 cups celery, in 1" slices
- 6 cups water
- Salt, optional
- Pepper, optional

Directions: Combine all the vegetables together in a large pot. Add the water and bring to a boil. Lower the heat and simmer for 5 minutes. Season with some salt and pepper.
Pour the soup into sterile jars, leaving 1-inch headspace. Wipe the jar rims clean and adjust the lids.
Process the filled jars in a pressure canner for 55 minutes at 10 pounds for a pressure canner with a weighted gauge or 11 pounds if the pressure canner has a dial gauge.

Nutrition: Calories: 206.8; Fat: 7.9g; Fiber: 1.8g; Carbs: 7.9g; Protein: 6.2g

129. Aztec Chicken Soup

Preparation Time: 15 minutes
Cooking Time: 2 hours & 25 minutes
Servings: 6 Pints

Ingredients:
- 1 poblano pepper, large
- 1-2 jalapeño peppers
- 6 tomatillos, fresh, husks removed
- 1½ cups white onion, chopped
- 1 tsp. cumin, ground
- 2 tbsp. olive oil
- 4 ears fresh corn
- 3 garlic cloves, minced
- 4 cups chicken stock/bone broth
- 2/3 cup lime juice, fresh
- 1½ tsp salt
- 1 tsp. black pepper, ground
- 1½ lb. chicken thighs/breasts, skinned and boned, cut into 1-inch chunks

Directions: Preheat the oven at 220°C. Take a baking sheet with aluminum foil and align poblano, jalapeno, and tomatillos.
Bake for 25 minutes or more until they become soft and the skin is blistered. Turn pepper every 5 minutes.
Remove peppers. Transfer in a bowl. Cover with plastic wrap and leave it for 20 minutes.
Cool tomatillos, chop them coarsely, and transfer them to a bowl. After 20 minutes, peel, seed, and chop peppers. Add tomatillos.
In a Stainless-steel Dutch oven, add olive oil and sauté onion and cumin on medium-high flame until softened.
In a large bowl, cut corn kernels tips. Scrape milk and pulp from corncobs. Add corn and garlic in the Dutch oven with onions and cook for 5 minutes with continuous stirring.
Add peppers, tomatillos, stock, lime juice, salt, and black pepper. Boil the mixture on a high flame.
Reduce flame and let it simmer, uncovered for 5 minutes with frequent stirring. Add chicken, boil on high flame for 5 minutes and stir. Remove from flame.
Transfer hot soup in hot jars. Leave headspace of 1-inch. Remove air bubbles. Clean the rim of the glass jar. Place the lid and apply a band around it. Adjust to ensure that the lid is tight.
In a pressure canner, place jars on racks with simmering water (2-inches, 90°C/180°F).
Place lid on canner, adjust medium-high heat. Vent steam for 10 minutes at 10/11 pounds (psi for weighted gauge/dial-gauge canner).
Process pint jars for 75 minutes or quarts for 90 minutes. Turn off the canner, remove the lid after two minutes when pressure turns zero. Keep the jars in the canner for 10 minutes more.
Remove the jars. Reprocess if the jars are not sealed. Cool and store in the refrigerator.

Nutrition: Calories: 69.8; Carbs: 7.9g; Fat: 2.8g; Protein: 5.2g

130. Black Bean Soup

Preparation Time: 15 minutes
Cooking Time: 2 hours & 10 minutes
Servings: 5 pints

Ingredients:
- 1 lb. black beans, dried
- 4 carrots, diced
- 2 onions, one-finely diced, one-halved
- 1 poblano pepper, seeded, diced
- 3 garlic cloves, minced
- 2 cups ham, diced
- 10 cups chicken stock
- 2 tsp cumin, ground
- 1½ tsp black pepper, freshly ground
- 3 tsp kosher salt
- 2 tsp oregano
- ½ tsp cayenne pepper

Directions: In a large bowl, add washed beans and soak in 3 inches of water. Drain. Rinse.
Put the beans in a pot with cold water covering around 3 inches. Add halved onion and bring it to a boil on high flame.
Lower the flame and let it simmer for 30 minutes. Strain beans and discard liquid and onion. Set aside.
In another pot, mix stock and all remaining ingredients. Let it simmer until thoroughly heated. Strain the mixture, reserve both stock and vegetables.
In each hot jar, fill ¼ of the jars with beans, ¼ cup vegetables, and ham. Pour stock over them. Leave headspace of 1-inch. Remove air bubbles.
Clean the rim of the glass jar. Place the lid and apply a band around it. Adjust to ensure that the lid is tight.
In a pressure canner, place jars on racks with simmering water (2-inches, 90°C/180°F).
Place lid on canner, adjust medium-high heat. Vent steam for 10 minutes at 10/11 pounds (psi for weighted gauge/dial-gauge canner). Process pint jars for 75 minutes or quarts for 90 minutes.
Turn off the canner, remove the lid after two minutes when pressure turns zero. Keep the jars in the canner for 10 minutes more. Remove the jars. Reprocess if the jars are not sealed. Cool and store in the refrigerator.

Nutrition: Calories: 109.8; Carbs: 59.9g; Fat: 1.9g; Protein: 6.2g

131. Black Eyed-Pea Soup

Preparation Time: 15 minutes
Servings: 4 pints
Cooking Time: 2 hours & 15 minutes

Ingredients:
- 1 lb. black eyed-pea, soaked overnight
- 1 onion, medium-sized, chopped
- 4 garlic cloves
- 2 red bell peppers, charred, chopped
- 2 tomatoes, peeled, diced, remove skin by dipping in boiling water
- 2 carrots, peeled, thinly sliced
- 2 chicken breast cubes, cooked
- ½ tsp tabasco sauce
- ½ tsp liquid smoke
- 8 cups chicken stock
- ½ lb. chard
- 1 tsp black pepper
- 1 tbsp olive oil
- ½ cup white wine (optional)
- Salt to taste

Directions: Take a 4L pan, add soaked black eyed-pea, cover, and boil on high flame for 2 minutes. Remove from flame. Leave it for an hour. Drain. In the pan, add oil to sauté onion, garlic, and peppers until onions become soft. Now, add peas, tomatoes, carrots, chicken, sauce, smoke, stock, and wine. Cook it on a medium flame for 30 minutes.

Add chard and let it simmer for 10 minutes. Add chard leaves, pepper, and salt. Stir well. Remove from flame. Transfer hot soup in hot jars. Leave headspace of 1-inch. Remove air bubbles. Clean the rim of the glass jar. Place the lid and apply a band around it. Adjust to ensure that the lid is tight.

In a pressure canner, place jars on racks with simmering water (2-inches, 90°C/180°F).

Place lid on canner, adjust medium-high heat. Vent steam for 10 minutes at 10/11 pounds (psi for weighted gauge/dial-gauge canner).

Process pint jars for 75 minutes or quarts for 90 minutes. Turn off the canner, remove the lid after two minutes when pressure turns zero. Keep the jars in the canner for 10 minutes more.

Remove the jars. Reprocess if the jars are not sealed. Cool and store in the refrigerator.

Nutrition: Calories: 169.8; Carbs: 22.9g; Fat: 2.7g; Protein: 14.2g

132. Butter Squash Soup

Preparation Time: 15 minutes
Servings: 10-12 pints
Cooking Time: 1 hour & 15 minutes

Ingredients:
- 1 large/2 small butternut squashes, peeled, cubed
- 2 apples, peeled, sliced
- 2 red onions, peeled, sliced
- 5 carrots, medium-sized, peeled and sliced
- 2 sweet potatoes, peeled, cubed
- 3 tsp salt (optional)

Directions: In hot jars, layer squash, apple, onions, and carrots equally in all jars. Leave headspace of 1-inch. Add ¼ tsp in each jar, if desired.

Pour boiling water over vegetables and leave a headspace of 1-inch. Remove air bubbles. Clean the rim of the glass jar. Place the lid and apply a band around it. Adjust to ensure that the lid is tight.

In a pressure canner, place jars on racks with simmering water (2-inches, 90°C/180°F).

Place lid on canner, adjust medium-high heat. Vent steam for 10 minutes at 10/11 pounds (psi for weighted gauge/dial-gauge canner). Process pint jars for 75 minutes or quarts for 90 minutes.

Turn off the canner, remove the lid after two minutes when pressure turns zero. Keep the jars in the canner for 10 minutes more. Remove the jars. Reprocess if the jars are not sealed. Cool and store in the refrigerator.

Nutrition: Calories: 214.8; Carbs: 34.9g; Fat: 2.7g; Protein: 15.3g

133. Carrot and Fennel Soup

Preparation Time: 15 minutes
Servings: 12 pints
Cooking Time: 2 hours & 25 minutes

Ingredients:
- 2 kg (4 lbs.) carrots, peeled, sliced
- 1 lb. fennel bulb/celery, trimmed
- 1 tbsp olive oil
- 3 l vegetable stock
- 2 tbsp salt
- 2 tsp onion powder
- 1 tsp thyme, dried
- 1 tsp ginger, dried, ground
- 1 tsp coriander, dried, ground
- 1 tsp black pepper, ground
- ½ tsp cumin, dried, ground
- 3 tbsp lemon juice (fresh/bottled) optional

Directions: Take a 6L pot, heat olive oil, and sauté fennel/celery until translucent. Add carrots and 1L stock. Let it simmer for 30 minutes on medium-low flame. Cool the mixture.

Blend the mixture. Pour the puree back into the pot. Add 2L stock and bring it to boil then, lower the flame and let it simmer for 20-30 minutes. Add lemon juice for flavor, if desired.

Transfer the hot soup to hot jars. Leave headspace of 1-inch. Remove air bubbles. Clean the rim of the glass jar. Place the lid and apply a band around it. Adjust to ensure that the lid is tight.

In a pressure canner, place jars on racks with simmering water (2-inches, 90°C/180°F).

Place lid on canner, adjust medium-high heat. Vent steam for 10 minutes at 10/11 pounds (psi for weighted gauge/dial-gauge canner).

Process pint jars for 75 minutes or quarts for 90 minutes. Turn off the canner, remove the lid after two minutes when pressure turns zero. Keep the jars in the canner for 10 minutes more.

Remove the jars. Reprocess if the jars are not sealed. Cool and store in the refrigerator.

Nutrition: Calories: 292.7; Carbs: 42.9g; Fat: 13.9g; Protein: 3.2g

134. French Onion Soup

Preparation Time: 15 minutes **Cooking Time: 2 hours & 20 minutes**
Servings: 8 pints

Ingredients:
- 1 tbsp butter
- 4 lb. (2 kg) onions, thinly sliced
- 1 tbsp salt
- 1 tsp black pepper, ground
- 1 tsp thyme, dried
- 3 cups dry white wine
- 3 qt. (3 l) beef/chicken/vegetable broth, or commercial stock

Directions: In an 8L Stainless-steel Dutch oven, melt butter on medium-low flame. Add onion, salt, pepper, thyme, and 2 cups of wine. Cover it and cook for 60 minutes or more until onion becomes tender with frequent stirring.

Uncover, cook until onion turns caramel color. Add 1 cup of wine, cook for 2 minutes, stir, and bring it to a boil. Reduce flame and let it simmer uncovered for 15 minutes.

In hot jars, transfer the hot soup and leave a headspace of 1-inch. Remove air bubbles. Clean the rim of the glass jar. Place the lid and apply a band around it. Adjust to ensure that the lid is tight.

In a pressure canner, place jars on racks with simmering water (2-inches, 90°C/180°F).

Place lid on canner, adjust medium-high heat. Vent steam for 10 minutes at 10/11 pounds (psi for weighted gauge/dial-gauge canner).

Process pint jars for 60 minutes or quarts for 75 minutes. Turn off the canner, remove the lid after two minutes when pressure turns zero. Keep the jars in the canner for 10 minutes more.

Remove the jars. Reprocess if the jars are not sealed. Cool and store in the refrigerator.

Nutrition: Calories: 209.8; Carbs: 17.9g; Fat: 9.9g; Protein: 13.1g

135. Beef Bone Broth

Preparation Time: 15 minutes **Cooking Time: 8 hours & 50 minutes**
Servings: 4 pints

Ingredients:
- 4 lb. (2 kg) meaty beef bones
- 2 qt. (2 l) water
- 2 tbsp unfiltered apple cider vinegar (5% acidity)
- 2 tsp salt
- 3 garlic cloves, crushed
- 2 bay leaves
- 1 large onion, quartered

Directions: Preheat the oven at 200°C. In a large roasting pan, place beef bones and bake for 30 minutes. Removes bones.

Reduce temperature to 107°C. Place a Stainless-steel Dutch oven, add bones, pan drippings, water, vinegar, salt, garlic, bay leaves, and onion. Stir well. Cover and bake for 8 hours.

Reduce temperature to 90°C and bake 8 hours more. Remove bones. In a 2L bowl, strain the broth using a fine wire-mesh strainer. Skim fat and discard solids.

Add water if the broth doesn't measure 2L.

Pour broth in a large Dutch oven and let it simmer.

Transfer the broth to hot jars. Leave headspace of 1-inch. Clean the rim of the glass jar. Place the lid and apply a band around it. Adjust to ensure that the lid is tight.

In a pressure canner, place jars on racks with simmering water (2-inches, 90°C/180°F).

Place lid on canner, adjust medium-high heat. Vent steam for 10 minutes at 10/11 pounds (psi for weighted gauge/dial-gauge canner).

Process pint jars for 20 minutes or quarts for 25 minutes. Turn off the canner, remove the lid after two minutes when pressure turns zero. Keep the jars in the canner for 10 minutes more.
Remove the jars. Reprocess if the jars are not sealed. Cool and store in the refrigerator.

Nutrition: Calories: 50.9; Carbs: 2.8g; Fat: 0g; Protein: 8.2g

136. Chicken Bone Broth

Preparation Time: 15 minutes
Servings: 4 pints
Cooking Time: 14 hours & 20 minutes

Ingredients:
- 4-5 lb./2-2.25 kg carcass (including skin roast chicken, broken into large pieces)
- 2 l water
- 1 tbsp salt
- 1 tbsp unfiltered apple cider vinegar (5% acidity)
- 2 carrots, large, coarsely chopped
- 2 bay leaves
- 1 onion, large, coarsely chopped

Directions: Preheat the oven at 107°C. In a large Stainless-steel Dutch oven, add carcass, water, salt, vinegar, carrots, bay leaves, and onion. Cover and bake for 7 hours.
Reduce temperature to 90oC and bake for additional 7 hours. Remove bones. In a 2L bowl, strain the broth using a fine wire-mesh strainer. Skim fat and discard solids. Add water if the broth doesn't measure 2L.
Pour broth in a large Dutch oven and let it simmer. Transfer the broth to hot jars. Leave headspace of 1-inch. Clean the rim of the glass jar.
Place the lid and apply a band around it. Adjust to ensure that the lid is tight. In a pressure canner, place jars on racks with simmering water (2-inches, 90°C/180°F).
Place lid on canner, adjust medium-high heat. Vent steam for 10 minutes at 10/11 pounds (psi for weighted gauge/dial-gauge canner). Process pint jars for 20 minutes or quarts for 25 minutes.
Turn off the canner, remove the lid after two minutes when pressure turns zero. Keep the jars in the canner for 10 minutes more.

Nutrition: Calories: 79.9; Carbs: 0.8g; Fat: 0g; Protein: 7.1g

137. Chicken Stock

Preparation Time: 15 minutes
Servings: 8 pints
Cooking Time: 2 hours & 20 minutes

Ingredients:
- 3-4 pounds chicken pieces
- 4 quarts water
- 2 stalks celery, leaves attached, cut into 1-inch pieces
- 2 onions, medium-sized, quartered
- 15 peppercorns
- 3 bay leaves
- salt to taste

Directions: In a 6-8L Pot. Add chicken and water and bring it to boil on high flame. Add all remaining ingredients. Reduce heat and cover, and then let it simmer for 2 hours or until chicken becomes tender. Remove from flame. Skim foam. Remove chicken for other use.
Strain the stock through a mesh strainer or several layers of cheesecloth into a large bowl. Cool and refrigerate for easy removal of fat. Remove fat. Pour the stock into a pot and boil.
Transfer the stock to hot jars. Leave headspace of 1-inch. Clean the rim of the glass jar. Place the lid and apply a band around it. Adjust to ensure that the lid is tight.
In a pressure canner, place jars on racks with simmering water (2-inches, 90°C/180°F).
Place lid on canner, adjust medium-high heat. Vent steam for 10 minutes at 10/11 pounds (psi for weighted gauge/dial-gauge canner). Process pint jars for 20 minutes or quarts for 25 minutes.
Turn off the canner, remove the lid after two minutes when pressure turns zero. Keep the jars in the canner for 10 minutes more. Use the unsealed jars within a week.

Nutrition: Calories: 29.9; Carbs: 0.8g; Fat: 2.9g; Protein: 4.3g

138. Spicy Roasted Pork Broth

Preparation Time: 15 minutes
Servings: 6 pints

Cooking Time: 1 hour & 15 minutes

Ingredients:

- 3 lb. (1.5 kg) boneless pork shoulder, trimmed, cut in 1½-inch cubes
- 4 tsp salt
- ½ tsp black pepper, ground
- 1 tbsp canola oil
- 2 qt. (2 l) chicken bone broth
- 1 (8-oz./250-g) onion, halved vertically and cut crosswise into thin slices
- 2 tbsp red pepper, dried, crushed
- 1½ tbsp oregano, dried
- 3 garlic cloves, minced

Directions: Preheat the oven at 220°C. On an aluminum foil rimmed baking sheet, place pork and sprinkle black pepper and 1 tsp salt. Drizzle with oil and toss. Arrange in a single layer and bake for 30 minutes or until the pork turns brown. Meanwhile, take a 4L Stainless-steel Dutch oven, add broth, salt, onion, pepper, oregano, and garlic. Boil. Reduce flame, cover, and let it simmer for 5 minutes.

Transfer the broth in hot jars with pork cubes. Leave headspace of 1-inch. Clean the rim of the glass jar. Place the lid and apply a band around it. Adjust to ensure that the lid is tight.

In a pressure canner, place jars on racks with simmering water (2-inches, 90°C/180°F).

Place lid on canner, adjust medium-high heat. Vent steam for 10 minutes at 10/11 pounds (psi for weighted gauge/dial-gauge canner). Process pint jars for 75 minutes or quarts for 90 minutes.

Turn off the canner, remove the lid after two minutes when pressure turns zero. Keep the jars in the canner for 10 minutes more.

Nutrition: Calories: 49.9; Carbs: 1.8g; Fat: 0g; Protein: 10.1g

139. Creole Sauce

Preparation Time: 15 minutes
Servings: 64

Cooking Time: 45 minutes

Ingredients:

- 2½ pounds tomatoes, peeled, cored and chopped
- 1 cup onion, chopped
- ½ cup sweet red pepper
- ¼ cup celery, chopped
- 1 garlic clove, minced
- ½ red chili pepper, chopped
- ½ tbsp fresh parsley, minced
- ½ tbsp sugar
- 1 tsp salt
- ¼ tsp dried marjoram
- ¼ tsp red chili powder

Directions: In a stainless-steel saucepan, add all ingredients over medium-high heat and cook until boiling. Now set the heat to low and cook for about 40 minutes, stirring frequently.

In 4 (1-pint) hot sterilized jars, divide the sauce, leaving about ½-inch space from the top. Slide a small knife around the insides of each jar to remove air bubbles. Wipe any trace of food off the rims of jars with a clean, moist kitchen towel. Carefully place the jars in the pressure canner and process at 6 pounds pressure for about 35 minutes. Remove the jars from pressure canner and place onto a wood surface several inches apart to cool completely. After cooling with your finger, press the top of each jar's lid to ensure that the seal is tight. The canned sauce can be preserved in the pantry for up to 1 month.

Nutrition: Calories: 4.8; Fat: 0g; Carbs: 0.9g; Protein: 1.1g

140. Mango BBQ Sauce

Preparation Time: 15 minutes
Servings: 40

Cooking Time: 40 minutes

Ingredients:

- 2 tbsps canola oil
- 2 medium onions, chopped
- 2 large garlic cloves, minced
- 3 cups tomatoes, peeled and chopped
- ½ cup dry red wine
- 3 tbsps honey
- 1 tbsp cider vinegar
- 1 tbsp Worcestershire sauce
- 1 tsp dry mustard
- 1 tsp whole peppercorns
- 1 tsp chipotle pepper powder
- 1½ tsps kosher salt
- ¼ cup water
- ¼ cup mango jam
- 2 tbsps brown sugar
- ½ tsp chipotle pepper hot sauce

Directions: In a nonreactive saucepan, heat the canola oil over medium-high heat and sauté the onions and garlic for about 5 minutes, stirring occasionally.

Add the tomatoes, wine, honey, vinegar, Worcestershire sauce, mustard, peppercorns, chili powder, and salt and bring to a boil.

Now adjust the heat and simmer for about 30 minutes. Remove the pan of sauce from heat and set aside to cool slightly.

In a blender, add tomato mixture and pulse until smooth. Return the sauce into the same pan over medium heat. Stir in the water, jam, brown sugar, and hot sauce and cook until boiling.

In 5 (½-pint) hot sterilized jars, divide the sauce, leaving about ½-inch space from the top.

Slide a small knife around the insides of each jar to remove air bubbles. Wipe any trace of food off the rims of jars with a clean, moist kitchen towel.

Carefully place the jars in the pressure canner and process at 6 pounds pressure for about 35 minutes.

Remove the jars from pressure canner and place onto a wood surface several inches apart to cool completely.

After cooling with your finger, press the top of each jar's lid to ensure that the seal is tight. The canned sauce can be preserved in the pantry for up to 1 month.

Nutrition: Calories: 25.8; Fat: 0.7g; Carbs: 4.1g; Protein: 0.4g

CHAPTER 6: BONUS RECIPES

141. Balsamic Tomato Jam
Preparation Time: 10 minutes
Cooking Time: 30 minutes
Servings: 2 pints

Ingredients:
- 2 pounds tomatoes, diced
- 1 teaspoon kosher salt
- ½ cup rosemary, freshly chopped
- 2 tablespoons brown sugar
- 2 teaspoons freshly ground black pepper
- ¼ cup balsamic vinegar

Directions: Add the tomatoes to a medium-size pot and cook over medium-low heat for 10 minutes.
Once the tomatoes start releasing the liquid, add the remaining ingredients and lower the heat to low.
Continue cooking for 20 minutes, or until the mixture reaches a jam-like consistency.
Pour into 4 half-pint jars and seal tightly. Refrigerate.

Nutrition: Calories: 19.8; Protein: 0.5g; Carbs: 3.9g; Fat: 0g

142. Ginger Nectarine Jam
Preparation Time: 20 minutes
Cooking Time: 50 minutes
Canning Time: 10 minutes
Servings: 6 half-pint jars

Ingredients:
- 5 pounds nectarines, ripe and firm
- 3 cups sugar
- 4 tablespoons lemon juice, freshly squeezed
- 2 tablespoons ginger, minced
- 1 tablespoon fresh ginger, freshly grated
- 2 teaspoons ground ginger

Directions: Fill a large pot with water, set a metal rack on top, and place the nectarines on top.
Bring to a boil until the skins loosen and transfer them to a baking sheet to cool.
Once cooled, peel, and dice the nectarines into 1/2-inch pieces.
Next, transfer them to a saucepan and add all the other ingredients.
Bring to a boil for 40 minutes over moderately high heat, ensuring everything dissolves.
Once ready, remove the mixture and carefully ladle it into the jars, leaving ¼ inch at the top.
Clean the rims, close tightly, and boil for 10 minutes in a hot-water canner.
Remove the jars, allow them to cool, and refrigerate.

Nutrition: Calories: 37.9; Protein: 1.2g; Carbs: 4.8g; Fat: 0g

143. Ground Turkey Taco Salad
Preparation Time: 15 minutes
Cooking Time: 20 minutes
Servings: 6

Ingredients:
- ½ pound ground turkey
- 1 tablespoon olive oil
- 1 teaspoon chili powder
- ½ cup shredded cheddar cheese
- ½ teaspoon cumin
- ¼ teaspoon garlic powder
- ¼ teaspoon salt
- ½ cup salsa
- 3 cups chopped romaine lettuce
- 2 tablespoons mashed avocado
- ½ teaspoon lemon juice
- 1 cup halved cherry tomatoes
- ½ cup whole-grain tortilla chips

Directions: Heat the olive oil in a sizable skillet over medium-high heat. Fry the ground turkey with chili powder, cumin, garlic powder, and salt until it is completely cooked.
Put on a clean bowl and let it cool completely.
In a small bowl, mix the mashed avocado with the lemon juice.
Spoon the salsa equally into 6 pint-sized canning jars, followed by the mashed avocado.
Next, layer the jars with cooled turkey, tomatoes, and lettuce, and top it off with the broken tortilla chips and shredded cheese.

Nutrition: Calories: 339.8; Fat: 7.9g; Fiber: 1.9g; Carbs: 7.7g; Protein: 6.2g

144. Fig & Pistachio Jam

Preparation Time: 20 minutes
Canning Time: 10 minutes
Cooking Time: 20 minutes
Servings: 6 half-pint jars

Ingredients:
- 3 pounds Black Mission figs, sliced into 1-inch pieces
- 4 cups sugar
- 2 oranges zest, finely grated
- 1 cup orange juice, freshly squeezed
- 4 tablespoons lemon juice, freshly squeezed
- 1 teaspoon cinnamon
- ½ teaspoons cloves, ground
- ¾ cup raw pistachios, shelled

Directions: In a large saucepan, mix the Black Mission figs, orange zest and juice, lemon juice, cinnamon, cloves, and sugar. Bring to a boil for 15 minutes until the liquid thickens.
Stir in the pistachios and continue cooking for 2 minutes.
Remove the mixture from the heat and ladle it into 6 half-pint jars.
Wipe the rims, close tightly, immerse in a hot water canner, and process for 10 minutes.
Once ready, remove the jars and let them cool, and refrigerate.

Nutrition: Calories: 65.8; Protein: 2.1g; Carbs: 7.9g; Fat: 0g

145. Dehydrated Candied Bacon

Preparation Time: 10 minutes
Servings: 10
Cooking Time: 12 hours dehydration

Ingredients:
- 1-pound bacon, thinly sliced
- 2 cups sugar
- ¾ cup water
- 1 tablespoon lemon juice

Directions: Combine your sugar and water lemon juice into a stock pan and bring to a boil for about 5 minutes. Add in your bacon and set the strips on the dehydrator tray, place in the dehydrator, and leave to fully dry at 135°F for about 10–12 hours. Enjoy!

Nutrition: Calories: 101.8; Protein: 0g; Fat: 0g; Carbs: 26.8g

146. Soy Marinated Salmon Jerky

Preparation Time: 10 minutes
Servings: 2
Cooking Time: 3–4 hours dehydration

Ingredients:
- 1-pound boneless salmon fillet
- Salt and pepper to taste
- ½ cup apple cider vinegar
- 2 tablespoons low-sodium soy sauce
- 1 tablespoon fresh lemon juice
- 2 teaspoons paprika
- ½ teaspoon garlic powder

Directions: Freeze the salmon for about 30 minutes until it is firm.
Meanwhile, whisk together the apple cider vinegar, soy sauce, and lemon juice in a mixing bowl.
Add the paprika and garlic powder then stir well.
Season the salmon with salt and pepper to taste, then remove the skin.
Slice the salmon into ¼-inch thick strips, then place them in a bowl or glass dish.
Pour in the marinade, turning to coat, and then cover with plastic and chill for 12 hours.
Drain the salmon slices and place them on paper towels to soak up the extra liquid.
Spread the salmon slices on your dehydrator trays in a single layer.
Dry for 3 to 4 hours at 145°F (63°C) until it is dried but still tender and chewy.
Cool the salmon jerky completely, then store in airtight containers in a cool, dark location.

Nutrition: Calories: 202.8; Protein: 0g; Fat: 0g; Carbs: 26.9g

147. Teriyaki Beef Jerky

Preparation Time: 10 minutes
Servings: 2
Cooking Time: 4 hours dehydration

Ingredients:
- 2 ½ to 3 pounds boneless beef sirloin
- Salt and pepper to taste
- ¼ cup low-sodium soy sauce
- ¼ cup light brown sugar, packed
- 2 tablespoons liquid smoke

- *1 teaspoon cider vinegar*

Directions: Whisk together the soy sauce, sugar, liquid smoke, and cider vinegar in a mixing bowl.
Trim the fat from the beef and cut it into ¼-inch thick strips.
Season the beef with salt and pepper to taste, then add to the bowl with the marinade.
Toss to coat, then cover with plastic and chill for 24 hours.
Spread the meat slices on your dehydrator trays in a single layer.
Dry for 4 hours at 145 °F (63 °C) until it is dried but still tender and chewy.
Cool the jerky completely, and then store it in airtight containers in a cool, dark location.

Nutrition: Carbs: 31.9g; Fat: 10.9g; Protein: 24.3g; Calories: 297.9

148. Mango Jalapeño Jam

Preparation Time: 10 minutes　　**Cooking Time: 30 minutes**
Canning Time: 10 minutes　　**Servings: 2 half-pint jars**

Ingredients:
- 4 whole mangoes, ripe
- 6 whole Jalapeno, seeded and stemmed
- ½–1 cup apple cider vinegar
- ¼ cup lemon juice, freshly squeezed
- 3 cups sugar
- 3 ounces powder pectin

Directions: In a medium bowl, crush the mangoes with a potato masher and process the jalapeños and vinegar using a food processor until fine. Next, combine all the other ingredients except pectin in a saucepan and simmer for 30 minutes, stirring constantly. Stir in the pectin powder and boil for 1 minute.
Remove the heat immediately and skim the foam. Carefully ladle into the pint jars and process in a boiling water canner for 10 minutes. Remove, let the jam cool, and refrigerate.

Nutrition: Calories: 32.8; Protein: 3.2g; Carbs: 6.8g; Fat: 0g

149. Split Pea Soup

Preparation Time: 15 minutes　　**Cooking Time: 1 hour and 30 minutes**
Canning Time: 90 minutes　　**Servings: 2**

Ingredients:
- 1-pound yellow, dry split peas
- 2 quarts water
- 4 teaspoons lime juice
- ¾ cups peeled and sliced carrots
- 1 cup peeled and chopped onions
- 2 garlic cloves peeled, minced
- ½ teaspoon cayenne pepper
- 1 teaspoon cumin seed and coriander
- 1 teaspoon salt

Directions: Allow the water with split peas in it to come to boil in a large stockpot.
Let it gently simmer without cover until the peas become soft; this will take about an hour.
Add the remaining ingredients and allow it to continue simmering for 30 minutes more.
Check the consistency and thin out the water if necessary. Ladle it into jars and leave a headspace of 1 inch.
Put a lid on and seal. Put it in a canner with hot water of 2–3 inches and allow it to process for 90 minutes at high pressure.

Nutrition: Calories: 157.9; Fat: 2.7g; Carbs: 25.8g; Protein: 8.5g

150. Onion Jam

Preparation Time: 15 minutes　　**Cooking Time: 30 minutes**
Canning Time: 10 minutes　　**Servings: 2 half-pint jars**

Ingredients:
- ¼ cup vegetable oil
- 4 large red onions, sliced
- 2 cups dry red wine
- Kosher salt and freshly ground black pepper
- Gastrique:
- ½ cup honey
- ½ cup red wine vinegar
- 1 lemon juice and a pinch of zest, optional

Directions: In a medium sauté pan, add the oil and heat until it begins to lightly smoke. Add the salt, onions, and pepper, and cook for 5 minutes.
Pour in the red wine and lower the heat to simmer until the wine almost evaporates completely.

In the meantime, start preparing your gastrique by heating the honey in a separate pan until it turns a light caramel color.
Put the red wine vinegar and simmer on low heat for 7 minutes, and then shut off the heat. Transfer the honey mixture into the onion mixture and continue cooking over low heat for 15 minutes.
Put the lemon juice and zest and remove the heat immediately and skim the foam.
Carefully ladle into the pint jars and process in a boiling water canner for 10 minutes.
Remove, let the jam cool, and refrigerate.

Nutrition: Calories 77.9; Protein: 2.1g; Carbs: 3.9g; Fat: 0g

151. Jalapeno Fish

Preparation Time: 20 minutes
Servings: 5 pints
Cooking Time: 1 hour and 30 minutes

Ingredients:
- 5 pounds tuna or salmon
- 5-pint sized Mason jars with lids and rings
- 1 tps. Canning salt
- 2 tps. Lemon juice
- 1 jalapeño pepper

Directions: Place 1 slice of jalapeño pepper into each jar. Fill jars with meat to 1/2 inch from the top.
Add 1/4 teaspoon of canning salt and 1 teaspoon of lemon juice per pint.
Use a knife to jiggle meat and remove any air pockets. Wipe rim of jar clean.
Heat the lids in hot water for 3 minutes; place the lids on jars and tighten rings slightly.
Put the jars in the canner and fill with water to the jar rings.
Close and lock the pressure canner and bring to a boil over high heat, then add cooking weight to the top.
After 20 minutes, turn the heat to medium and cook for 75 minutes.
Turn off the heat and leave the canner alone until it has cooled completely to room temperature.
After the canner has cooled, remove the jars from the canner and check for sealing.
If jars have sealed, store for up to 2 years; if not, use the meat right away.

Nutrition: Carbs: 1.4g; Fat: 32.3g; Protein: 93.9g; Calories: 699.8

152. Red Pepper Jam

Preparation Time: 20 minutes
Canning Time: 10 minutes
Cooking Time: 1 hour
Servings: 1 half-pint jar

Ingredients:
- 8 sweet red peppers, halved and seeded
- 2 tablespoons salt
- 1 cup red wine vinegar
- 2 cups sugar
- 1 dash cayenne pepper

Directions: Put the red peppers in a food processor and grind them coarsely.
Transfer them into a mixing bowl, season with salt, and cover with plastic wrap for 2 hours.
Once the 2 hours elapse, drain off half the liquid and add in the remaining ingredients.
Put in a saucepan and broil to a boil and then reduce the heat to a simmer.
Cook for 1 hour until the mixture has thickened, stirring occasionally.
Carefully ladle into the pint jars and process in a boiling water canner for 10 minutes.
Remove, let the jam cool, and refrigerate.

Nutrition: Calories: 13.8; Protein: 0.3g; Carbs: 0.1g; Fat: 0g

153. Banana & Pineapple Butter

Preparation Time: 10 minutes
Canning Time: 5 minutes
Cooking Time: 10 minutes
Servings: 4 half-pint jars

Ingredients:
- 1 cup banana (mashed)
- 1 cup canned crushed pineapple (with juice)
- 2 tablespoons maraschino cherries (chopped)
- 2 teaspoons lemon juice (fresh)
- 3 ½ cups granulated sugar
- 3 ounces liquid pectin

Directions: Sterilize the jars. Combine all the mentioned ingredients except the pectin in a saucepan and bring to a boil, stirring continuously. Leave to boil for a minute.

Turn off the flame, stir in the pectin for 5 minutes. Skim off any visible foam.
Ladle the mix immediately into the sterilized jars, leaving a quarter-inch of headspace.
Eliminate air bubbles and clean the rims. Cover the jars with the lid and apply the bands. Submerge the jars within a prepared boiling water canner for 5 minutes. Remove, allow them to cool, and then label the jars.

Nutrition: Calories: 115.8

154. Soft Cheese
Preparation Time: 10 minutes　　　　　　　　　　　　　　　　　　　　**Canning Time: 40 minutes**
Servings: 9 half-pint jars

Ingredients:
- 1 pound Velveeta cheese
- 5 ounces canned evaporated milk
- ½ teaspoon salt
- 1 tablespoon vinegar
- ½ teaspoon dry mustard

Directions: Sterilize the jars. Melt the cheese and milk in a double boiler and then mix in the remaining ingredients. Ladle the mix immediately into the sterilized jars, up to three-fourths full.
Eliminate air bubbles and clean the rims. Cover the jars with the lid and apply the bands. Submerge the jars within a prepared boiling water canner for 40 minutes. Remove, allow it to cool, and then label the jars.

Nutrition: Calories:188.7

155. Peachy Rum Conserve
Preparation Time: 15 minutes　　　　　　　　　　　　　　　　　　　　**Cooking Time: 30 minutes**
Canning Time: 15 minutes　　　　　　　　　　　　　　　　　　　　　　**Servings: 2-pint jars**

Ingredients:
- 3 tablespoons orange rind
- 2/3 cup orange pulp
- ½ cup maraschino cherries (chopped)
- ½ cup light rum
- 6 ½ cups sugar
- 2 cups peaches (peeled, pitted, chopped)
- ½ teaspoon ginger
- ¼ teaspoon mace
- ¾ cup pineapple (crushed)
- 3 tablespoons lemon juice
- ½ teaspoon salt

Directions: Sterilize the jars.
Mix together the orange pulp and orange rind in a pan and just cover with water, cooking until the rind is tender. Place the rum container in hot water and place it aside. Mix the pineapple, peaches, lime juice, and cherries in a pot along with the orange mix, then mix in the spices and sugar, stirring until the sugar dissolves.
Cook until it thickens, stirring frequently, then remove from heat and mix in the rum. Skim off any visible foam and ladle the mix immediately into the sterilized jars. Leave a quarter-inch of headspace, get rid of any air bubbles, and clean the rims. Cover the jars with the lid and apply the bands.
Submerge the jars within a prepared boiling water canner for 15 minutes.
Remove, allow it to cool, and then label the jars.

Nutrition: Calories: 219.8

156. Spiced Pear Butter
Preparation Time: 25 minutes　　　　　　　　　　　　　　　　　　　　**Cooking Time: 15 minutes**
Canning Time: 15 minutes　　　　　　　　　　　　　　　　　　　　　　**Servings: 9 half-pint jars**

Ingredients:
- 15 Bartlett pears (sliced)
- 1 teaspoon cloves (ground)
- 1 ½ teaspoons cinnamon (ground)
- 2 cups water
- 2 tablespoons lemon juice
- 6 cups sugar
- ½ teaspoon ginger (ground)

Directions: Sterilize the jars. Combine water and pears in a pan and cook covered until tender (approx. 30 minutes). Press the tender pears in a colander and then measure 8 cups of pear pulp.
Transfer the pear pulp back into the pan.
In a separate pan caramelize 1 ½ cups of water, stirring, and then transfer it into the pear pulp.
Combine in the rest of the ingredients except for the lemon juice and cook for around 45 minutes uncovered till thickened, stirring frequently. Switch off the flame and skim off any visible foam. Ladle the mix immediately into the sterilized jars, leaving a quarter-inch of headspace. Eliminate air bubbles and clean the rims.

Cover the jars with the lid and apply the bands. Submerge the jars within a prepared boiling water canner for 15 minutes. Remove, allow them to cool, and then label the jars.

Nutrition: Calories: 87.9

157. Rhubarb Compote with Ginger

Preparation Time: 10 minutes　　**Cooking Time: 15 minutes**
Servings: 4

Ingredients:
- 1 pound chopped rhubarb
- ½ cup orange juice
- 1 ½ cups sugar, or more
- 2 tablespoons chopped candied ginger

Directions: In a large glass or ceramic jar, mix the candied ginger, orange juice, sugar, and rhubarb. Let it stand overnight or for a minimum of 8 hours.
Pour the rhubarb mixture into a pot to boil for about 15 minutes over medium-low heat. Use sugar to sweeten and transfer it to a clean jar. Use a lid to cover well and put it into the refrigerator to store for up to 1 week.

Nutrition: Calories: 337.9

158. Kale Slaw

Preparation Time: 30 minutes　　**Cooking Time: 1 week**
Servings: 4

Ingredients:
- 3 cups kale leaves
- 2 carrots
- 1 cup small broccoli florets
- ½ medium onion
- Starter culture (optional)
- 1 tablespoon unrefined sea salt
- Filtered water

Directions: Wash the vegetables. Cleave or shred the kale leaves. Shred the carrots. Cut the broccoli florets into little pieces. Dice the onion. Put all the vegetables in a glass bowl and combine them.
Create brine by mixing the sea salt with 4 cups of sifted water and mixing the salt in until it dissolves. Include the starter culture now in case you're going to utilize it. Put the vegetables in the fermenting compartment. Pack them in firmly. Pour the brine into the compartment until it's directly over the top of the vegetables.
Place a load in the container and also press it down to squeeze any air pockets out of the vegetables. The brine ought to be over the top of the load when you're finished squeezing it down. Ensure you leave several inches of headspace at the head of the container because the salt in the saline solution will haul more moisture out of the vegetables.
Place the cover or lid on the container and let it ferment at room temperature for as long as seven days. Check it the following week and move it to the ice chest if you are satisfied with the fermentation. If not, let it ferment until you feel it's prepared.

Nutrition: Calories: 5.8

159. Lemon-Lime-Orange Marmalade

Preparation Time: 55 minutes　　**Cooking Time: 40 minutes**
Canning Time: 10 minutes　　**Servings: 5 half-pint jars**

Ingredients:
- 3 medium oranges
- 1 medium lemon
- 1 medium lime
- 1 ½ cups water
- 5 cups sugar
- ⅛ teaspoon baking soda
- 1 pouch liquid fruit pectin

Directions: Score the oranges, lemon, and lime peels into 4 lengthwise sections, peel, and scrape off the white portions. Slice the peels into thin strips and toss them into a large saucepan, add water, baking soda, and boil for 20 minutes.
In the meantime, section the oranges, lemon, and lime, ensuring you catch all the juices in a bowl and toss them into the boiling water. Continue to simmer for 10 minutes.
In a separate 10-quart heavy pot, add the sugar and fruit mixture, and boil for 10 minutes, stirring constantly. Next, quickly stir in pectin and continue to boil for 1 minute, stirring constantly.
Remove from heat, skim off foam, and ladle into the jars, leaving 1/4-inch headspace.
Wipe jar rims, screw bands, and process in a boiling-water canner for 10 minutes.

Remove the jars and cool on wire racks for several hours.

Nutrition: Calories: 51.8; Protein: 3.2g; Carbs: 12.9g; Fat: 0g

160. Apricot Amaretto Jam
Preparation Time: 30 minutes
Canning Time: 10 minutes
Cooking Time: 10 minutes
Servings: 8 half-pints

Ingredients:
- 4 ¼ cups peeled, crushed apricots
- ¼ cup lemon juice
- 6 ¼ cups sugar, divided
- 1 package powdered fruit pectin
- ½ teaspoon unsalted butter
- ⅓ cup amaretto

Directions: In a Dutch oven, combine lemon juice and apricots.
In a small bowl, mix pectin and ¼ cup of sugar. Stir into the apricot mixture and add butter. Broil to a full boil over medium-high heat, stirring constantly. Add the remaining sugar and let boil 1–2 minutes, stirring constantly. Remove from heat and stir in amaretto. Let the jam sit for 5 minutes, mixing occasionally.
Divide the hot mixture between 8 hot sterilized half-pint jars, leaving a ¼-inch space at the top. Wipe the rims carefully. Put tops on jars and screw on bands until fingertip tight.
Place jars into a canner with boiling water, ensuring that they are completely covered with water. Let boil for 10 minutes. Remove jars and cool.

Nutrition: Carbs: 20.8g; Fat: 0g; Protein: 0g; Calories: 85.7

161. Balsamic Vinegar-Ruby Port Jelly
Preparation Time: 30 minutes
Canning Time: 10 minutes
Cooking Time: 20 minutes
Servings: 8 half-pint jars

Ingredients:
- ¾ cup balsamic vinegar
- ½ cup orange peel, coarsely shredded
- 6 cups sugar
- 4 cups ruby port
- 1 3-ounce liquid fruit pectin

Directions: Combine vinegar and orange peel in a saucepan and bring to a boil for 10 minutes.
Reduce the heat and simmer uncovered for 5 minutes and remove from the heat. Let the mixture cool and sieve using a fine mesh and discard the peel. In a large pot combine the port, reduced vinegar, and sugar, and boil over high heat, stirring constantly. Toss in the pectin quickly and continue boiling for 2 minutes, stirring constantly. Remove from the heat and skim off the foam with a spoon.
Pour the jelly into hot sterilized half-pint jars, ensuring you leave 1/4-inch headspace.
Wipe jar rims, close the lids, and screw the bands.
Immerse in a boiling-water canner and process for 10 minutes.
Remove jars from the canner and cool.

Nutrition: Calories: 49.7; Protein: 2.1g; Carbs: 10.8g; Fat: 0g

162. Jasmine Tea Jelly
Preparation Time: 5 minutes
Canning Time: 10 minutes
Cooking Time: 15 minutes
Servings: 6 half-pint jars

Ingredients:
- 4 cups water
- 1 tablespoon fresh ginger, minced
- ¼ cup jasmine green tea
- 1 (1.75-ounce) powdered fruit pectin
- ¼ cup lemon juice
- 5 cups sugar

Directions: Combine the water and ginger in a medium saucepan and bring to a boil.
Reduce the heat and simmer covered for 5 minutes. Remove from the heat and stir in the jasmine green tea.
Cover and continue boiling for 5 minutes. Next, pour the ginger mixture through a fine-mesh sieve and discard the solids. Take 3 ½ cups of the liquid and transfer it to a large saucepan.
Stir in the fruit pectin and lemon juice, and continue boiling for 2 minutes.
Pour in the sugar and boil for 1 minute, stirring constantly.
Remove from heat, skim off the foam, and ladle into sterilized jars, leaving 1/4-inch headspace.

Wipe the rims, close the lids, and process the jars in a boiling-water canner for 10 minutes. Remove from the canner, let it cool, and refrigerate.

Nutrition: Calories: 43.9; Protein: 2.1g; Carbs: 11.8g; Fat: 0g

163. Vanilla Pear Berry Jam

Preparation Time: 25 minutes
Servings: 6 half-pint jars
Cooking Time: 20 minutes

Ingredients:
- 2 medium chopped pears
- 1 ½ tablespoon vanilla extract
- 3 cups fresh strawberries, hulled
- 5 cups sugar
- 1 package powdered fruit pectin
- 3 tps. Lemon juice

Directions: Add the crushed strawberries, lemon juice, pectin, and pears to a saucepan.
Toss in the oven and cook over medium heat, ensuring you stir continuously until it boils.
Add sugar and continue boiling for 1 minute while constantly stirring.
Remove from heat, scoop the foam, and add vanilla extract. In a jar, ladle hot mixture leaving 1/4-inch headspace. Remove air bubbles and tighten the lids.
Put jars in a canner, completely cover with water, and boil.
Process for 9 minutes, cool, and refrigerate.

Nutrition: Calories: 90.8; Protein: 0g; Carbs: 22.7g; Fat: 0g

164. Apple Pie Jam

Preparation Time: 20 minutes
Canning Time: 10 minutes
Cooking Time: 20 minutes
Servings: 6 half-pint jars

Ingredients:
- 1 cup water
- 5 cups sugar
- ½ teaspoon butter
- 4 large Golden Delicious apples, peeled and sliced
- 3 ounces liquid fruit pectin
- 1 ½ teaspoon ground cinnamon
- 1 teaspoon ground nutmeg
- ¼ teaspoon ground mace

Directions: In a Dutch oven, mix the apples and water. Cover and cook over medium heat until the apples are tender.
Add butter and sugar, and bring the mixture to a rolling boil over high heat, stirring continuously.
Stir in the pectin. Allow the mixture to boil for 1 minute while stirring.
Remove from heat and skim off foam. Stir in the spices.
Carefully pack the mixture into hot jars, leaving ¼ inch of space at the top.
Run a knife or spatula along the top to remove air bubbles.
Clean the rims of the jars, and screw on the lids and rings. Process in boiling water for 10 minutes.
Remove the jars and cool.

Nutrition: Calories: 198.7; Fat: 1.9g; Carbs: 13.8g; Fiber: 3.9g; Protein: 8.2g

165. Peach Mango Jam

Preparation Time: 20 minutes
Canning Time: 15 minutes
Cooking Time: 15 minutes
Servings: 6 half-pint jars

Ingredients:
- 2 pounds peaches, peeled and chopped
- 2 cups mangoes, peeled and chopped
- 5 cups sugar
- ¼ cup lemon juice
- 3 ounces liquid fruit pectin (half a small pouch)

Directions: Place peaches and lemon juice in a large pot and heat.
Crush the peaches with a potato masher until pulpy. Add the mangoes and sugar.
As soon as the mixture boils, stir in pectin. Boil for one minute, stirring constantly.
Remove from heat. Spoon into hot jars and wipe down the rims.
Screw on lids and bands and process in boiling water for 15 minutes. Remove and cool.

Nutrition: Calories: 174.8; Fat: 0g; Carbs: 14.9g; Fiber: 4.9g; Protein: 23.1g

166. Honey Blueberry Cobbler Jam

Preparation Time: 20 minutes
Servings: 4 half-pint jars

Cooking Time: 25 minutes

Ingredients:
- 1 teaspoon ground nutmeg
- 1 teaspoon vanilla extract
- ½ teaspoon ground cinnamon
- 1-ounce pectin
- 1 cup honey
- 4 ½ cups blueberries
- 1 ½ cups apple juice

Directions: Add mashed blueberries, pectin, and apple juice in a saucepan and stir.
Toss in the oven and bring to a boil over high heat, stirring constantly.
Stir in the nutmeg, honey, and cinnamon, and continue boiling for 2 minutes.
Remove from the oven and add the vanilla extract. Pour the jam in containers 1/2-inch to the brim.
Wipe the containers' edges and tightly cover immediately with lids.
Cool at room temperature for 24 hours then refrigerate.

Nutrition: Calories: 38.7; Protein: 0g; Carbs: 9.8g; Fat: 0g

167. Cherry Jam

Preparation Time: 25 minutes
Servings: 5 half-pints jars

Cooking Time: 20 minutes

Ingredients:
- 5 cups sugar
- 1 package powdered fruit pectin
- 1 teaspoon butter
- 2 pounds pitted tart cherries

Directions: In a processor, finely chop cherries. Put on an oven and add pectin and butter.
Stir constantly and broil to a boil over high heat. Stir in sugar and boil for 1 minute.
Skim off foam off the heat. Add the mixture into half-pint jars and leave 1/4-inch headspace.
Remove air bubbles and tighten the bands. Put jars in a canner with hot water and cover.
After boiling, process for 7 minutes in a water canner and allow it to cool. Refrigerate.

Nutrition: Calories: 88.9; Protein: 0g; Carbs: 22.8g; Fat: 0g

168. Mango Jam

Preparation Time: 10 minutes
Servings: 1 half-pint jar

Cooking Time: 20 minutes

Ingredients:
- 2 ripe mangoes
- 1 cup water
- 2 cups white sugar
- 2 saffron threads (optional)

Directions: Boil the mangoes until soft, cool, peel, and place in a medium mixing bowl.
Next, mash the mango mixture until smooth.
Add the mango mixture in a saucepan, 1 cup of water, sugar, and boil over low heat in an oven.
Once the mixture starts boiling, increase the heat to medium-high until the internal temperature reaches 135°C or until soft threads start to form. Add the saffron thread (optional) and boil the mixture for 6 minutes until it thickens. Cool the jam and pour in a jar and tighten the lid. Refrigerate.

Nutrition: Calories: 72.8; Protein: 0.4g; Carbs: 18.7g; Fat: 0.1g

169. Pineapple Jam

Preparation Time: 20 minutes
Servings: 2 half-pint jars

Cooking Time: 15 minutes

Ingredients:
- 1 medium ripe pineapple (finely diced)
- 1 ½ lemon (juiced)
- ¾ kg. sugar
- 2 mangoes (peeled, pureed, and strained)
- 5 cardamoms (crushed)

Directions: Add the pineapple, mango puree, lemons, sugar, and crushed cardamom to a boiling pot.

Boil over medium heat for 4 minutes ensuring you stir every 1 minute. Once done, remove from the heat, allow to cool, pour the jam into jars, and seal tightly. Cool while turned upside down and refrigerate.

Nutrition: Calories: 55.1; Protein: 0.3g; Carbs: 13.6g; Fat: 0g

170. Lemon Ginger Marmalade

Preparation Time: 30 minutes
Canning Time: 11 minutes
Cooking Time: 10 minutes
Servings: 5 half-pint jars

Ingredients:
- ½ teaspoon baking soda
- ½ cup coarsely grated fresh ginger
- 4 juicy lemons
- ½ teaspoon butter, unsalted
- ½ cup crystallized ginger
- 1.75 ounces powdered pectin
- 4 ½ cups granulated sugar

Directions: Peel the lemons, thinly slice them, toss in a heavy pot, add 2 cups of water, and boil over low heat for 4 minutes. In a separate bowl, squeeze the lemons and add to the boiling mixture.
Continue boiling for 1 minute, add butter, ginger, and pectin, ensuring you stir continuously.
Add sugar and boil for 2 more minutes as you stir. Put off the heat and add the crystallized ginger.
Skim foam from the mixture and pour it in clean jars leaving 1/4-inch space to the brim.
Put the jars in a pot full of water and boil for 11 minutes.
Remove the jars from the pot and allow the jam to rest overnight.

Nutrition: Calories: 137.9; Protein: 0.3g; Carbs: 35.1g; Fat: 0.1g

171. Peach Butter

Preparation Time: 10 minutes
Serving: 2 jars
Cooking Time: 30 minutes

Ingredients:
- 6 cups peaches, peeled, pitted, and chopped
- 1 teaspoon freshly squeezed lemon juice
- ½ teaspoon pure vanilla extract
- ¼ cup brown sugar or adjust to taste
- ½ teaspoon ground cinnamon

Directions: Combine the ingredients in a large saucepan over medium heat, stirring to ensure it doesn't stick to the bottom. After 30 minutes, when the peaches are completely soft, use a blender to puree the peaches to desired batter consistency. Once completely cooled, transfer to Mason jars, tightly seal and refrigerate.

Nutrition: Carbs: 187.9g; Fat: 1.3g; Protein: 2.5g; Calories: 715.8

172. Beef Stew

Preparation Time: 1 hour 57 minutes
Servings: 7 pints

Ingredients:
- 4-5 lb beef stew meat, cut into 1 1/2-inch cube
- 8 cups sliced carrots
- 3 cups chopped celery
- 1-1/2 tbsp. salt
- 1 tsp. Thyme
- ½ tsp. pepper
- Water
- 13 (16 oz.) pint glass preserving jars with lids
- 1 tbsp. vegetable oil
- 12 cups cubed and peeled potatoes
- 3 cups chopped onion

Directions: Set up a pressure canner. Warm jars in a saucepan of simmering water until ready to use. Avoid boiling. Clean lids with warm soapy water and set away bands.
In a large saucepot, brown the meat in oil. Season browned meat with veggies and seasonings. Submerge in hot water. Preheat oven to 350°F. Bring stew to a boil. Take the pan off the heat.
Fill hot jars halfway with stew, allowing a 1-inch headspace. Eliminate air bubbles. Wipe the rim. On the pot, center the hot lid. Apply band and tweak until it fits snugly around the fingertip.
Process filled pots in a pressure canner at a pressure of ten pounds. Pints take 1 hour and 15 minutes, and quarts take 1 hour and 30 minutes, adjusted for altitude. Turn off the heat and bring the good canner to zero pressure. Allow 5 minutes more before removing the lid. Let jars cool in the canner for ten minutes. Remove jars from heat and allow them to cool. After 24 hours, inspect coverings for seals. The top should not flex up and down when the center is squeezed.

173. Pears

Preparation Time: 30 minutes
Canning Time: 10 minutes
Cooking Time: 2 hours
Servings: 7 half-pints

Ingredients:
- 16 cups (16 medium-sized pears) peeled and sliced fresh pears
- 3 tablespoons lemon juice
- 2 cups water
- 4 cups sugar

Directions: Combine the four ingredients in a large kettle and bring to a boil.
Uncover, cook, and stir often for 1 ½ to 2 hours until consistent.
Remove from stove and ladle the hot preserves into prepared seven hot sterilized jars with ¼-inch headspace. Take out the air bubbles, make headspace adjustments, wipe the rims and place the lids on the jars, and screw on the bands. Place the jars in the boiling water in the canner and boil for 10 minutes. Remove the hot jars; let cool on top of a towel. Enjoy!

Nutrition: Carbs: 20.8g; Fat: 0g; Protein: 0g

174. African Curry

Preparation Time: 30 minutes
Servings: 3
Cooking Time: 35 minutes

Ingredients:
- 1 tablespoon olive oil
- 1 onion, chopped
- 2 garlic cloves, peeled and chopped
- 1 bay leaf
- 1 (14.5-ounce) can whole peeled tomatoes, drained
- 2 teaspoons curry powder
- 1/8 teaspoon salt
- 1 (2 to 3 pound) whole chicken, bones and skin removed, cut into pieces
- 1 (14-ounce) can unsweetened coconut milk
- 1 lemon, juiced

Directions: In a heavy, big skillet, heat olive oil on medium heat. Mix in bay leaf, garlic, and onion. Sauté until the onion is browned lightly. Mix salt, curry powder, and tomatoes in the skillet. Cook for about 5 minutes. Mix the chicken in. Cook until juices are clear and the chicken is not pink for 15–20 minutes.
Lower skillet heat down to low. Constantly stirring, blend in coconut milk gradually for around 10 minutes. Stir in lemon juice before serving.

Nutrition: Calories: 599.8; Fat: 33.3g; Carbs: 13.2g; Protein: 64.6g

175. Simple Tomato Sauce

Preparation Time: 10 minutes
Servings: 3
Cooking Time: 1 hour and 40 minutes

Ingredients:
- 2 teaspoons olive oil
- ½ cup minced onion
- 2 garlic cloves, crushed
- 1 (28-ounce) can crushed tomatoes
- 2 (6.5-ounce) cans canned tomato sauce
- 2 (6-ounce) cans tomato paste
- 1/2 cup water
- 2 tablespoons white sugar
- 2 tablespoons chopped fresh parsley
- 1 ½ teaspoon dried basil
- 1 tablespoon salt
- 1 teaspoon Italian seasoning
- ½ teaspoon fennel seeds
- ¼ teaspoon ground black pepper

Direction: In a big heavy pot, heat olive oil over medium heat. Cook and mix garlic and onion in the hot oil for 5 to 7 minutes until tender.
Mix water, canned tomato paste, tomato paste, and crushed tomatoes with the onion mixture until smooth. Put in pepper, fennel, Italian seasoning, salt, basil, parsley, and sugar then stir. Allow it to simmer then turn the heat to low. Cook for 1 to 1 ½ hour, occasionally stirring, until thick and the seasonings have permeated the sauce.

Nutrition: Calories: 85.8; Fat: 1.2g; Carbs: 17.5g; Protein: 3.7g

176. Greek Peas with Tomato and Dill

Preparation Time: 10 minutes
Servings: 3
Cooking Time: 40 minutes

Ingredients:
- 3 tablespoons olive oil
- 6 green onions, chopped
- 1 (16-ounce) package frozen peas
- 1 cup crushed tomatoes
- 1 potato, peeled and cut into wedges
- ½ cup chopped fresh dill
- ½ cup water (optional)
- Salt and ground black pepper to taste

Direction: In a saucepan, heat olive oil over medium heat and sauté onion for about 5 minutes until soft yet not browned. Add potato, tomatoes, peas, and dill; sprinkle with pepper and salt for seasoning. If there is not enough liquid from the tomatoes, add more water.

Mix well and bring to a boil. Reduce heat and cook, partly covered for about 30 minutes until potato and peas are tender. Make sure that all the liquid from the tomatoes has vaporized before serving.

Nutrition: Calories: 244.8; Carbs: 30.9g; Protein: 8.7g; Fat: 10.5g

177. Bottled Spaghetti Sauce

Preparation Time: 10 minutes
Canning Time: 45 minutes
Cooking Time: 2 hours
Servings: 3

Ingredients:
- 39 pounds fresh tomatoes, halved
- 3 pounds onions, halved
- 2 heads garlic cloves, peeled
- 2 cups olive oil
- 1 cup white sugar
- ½ cup salt
- 2 tablespoons dried oregano
- 1 tablespoon dried basil
- 6 (6-ounce) cans tomato paste, or as needed

Direction: Bring a big pot of water to boil then put in 14 one-quart jars; simmer to sterilize. Wash the rings and lids in warm soapy water.

In a blender, puree the tomatoes in batches until smooth then pour them into a big pot. Put the garlic and onions into the blender then puree until smooth; stir it into the pot.

In the pot, mix basil, oregano, salt, sugar, and olive oil then boil. Mix in tomato paste and simmer the sauce for about 2 hours, putting in more tomato paste if needed, until it becomes thick.

Pack the sauce into the hot and sterilized jars. Fill the jars to within 1/4 inch of the top. Remove food residue by wiping the jar rims with a damp paper towel. Put lids on and screw on rings.

Set a rack in a large stockpot's bottom and fill halfway with water. Boil then use a holder to lower the jars 2 inches apart into the boiling water. If necessary, add more boiling water to bring the water level to a minimum of 1 inch above the tops of the jars. Bring the water to a rolling boil then cover the pot. Process for 45 minutes.

Take the jars out of the stockpot then put them onto a wood or cloth-covered surface, several inches apart, for a minimum of 24 hours until cool. Ensure that the seal is tight by using a finger to press the top of each lid (lid must not move up or down).

Nutrition: Calories: 83.8; Fat: 4.1g; Carbs: 11.1g; Protein: 2.2g

178. Raspberry Peach Jam

Preparation Time: 35 minutes
Canning Time: 12 minutes
Cooking Time: 20 minutes
Servings: 2 half-pint jars

Ingredients:
- 2 cups chopped peaches
- 2 teaspoons lemon juice
- 4 cups raspberries
- 7 cups sugar

Directions: In a medium mixing bowl mix all ingredients. In the meantime, boil some water in a boiling-water canner. Transfer to a saucepan and put inside an oven. Cook over low heat for 16 minutes, stirring occasionally until the mixture becomes bubbly. Remove from the oven and carefully scoop off the foam.

Carefully pour in 2 250ml hot jars ensuring you leave a quarter-inch to the brim. Scoop bubbles if any.

Tightly close the lid and immerse the jar in the boiling-water canner for 12 minutes.

Once the 12 minutes elapses, remove the jar from the boiling water and leave to cool.

Nutrition: Calories: 65.8; Fat: 0g; Carbs: 15.8g; Fiber: 0g; Protein: 0g

179. Tri-Berry Jam

Preparation Time: 20 minutes
Canning Time: 10 minutes
Cooking Time: 10 minutes
Servings: 10 half-pint jars

Ingredients:
- 3 cups fresh or frozen red raspberries
- 3 cups fresh or frozen strawberries
- 3 ½ cups fresh or frozen blueberries
- 2 packages powdered fruit pectin
- ¾ cup lemon juice
- 12 cups sugar

Directions: In a stockpot, mix the lemon juice and berries and slightly crush.
Pour in a pan, stir in pectin and boil over high heat for 10 minutes, ensuring you stir constantly.
Add sugar and leave to boil for 1 minute and continue stirring. Remove from the heat and scoop off any foam.
Ladle the mixture into hot jars, ensuring you leave 1/4-inch headspace.
Scoop the bubbles and adjust the lids. In a boiling water canner, process the mixture for 10 minutes.
Leave to cool and enjoy.

Nutrition: Calories: 97.9; Fat: 0g; Carbs: 24.8g; Fiber: 0g; Protein: 0g

180. Pineapple Chipotle

Preparation Time: 20 minutes
Servings: 3 pints
Cooking Time: 10 minutes

Ingredients:
- 4 cups seeded papaya
- 2 cups chopped or cubed pineapples
- 1 cup raisins
- 1 cup lemon juice
- ½ cup lime juice
- ½ cup pineapple juice
- ½ cup Anaheim peppers
- 2 teaspoons chopped onions
- 2 teaspoons chopped cilantro
- 2 teaspoons brown sugar

Directions: Add together all 10 ingredients in a saucepan and bring to a boil, but you need to stir constantly. Reduce to a steady simmer and let thicken, but still stirring constantly. Add to the canning jars and seal.

Nutrition: Carbs: 59.9g; Fat: 0.8g; Protein: 2.4g; Calories: 232.8

181. Green Salsa

Preparation Time: 20 minutes
Servings: 3 pints
Cooking Time: 10 minutes

Ingredients:
- 7 cups chopped green tomatoes
- 3 cups chopped jalapenos
- 2 cups chopped red onions
- 2 teaspoons minced garlic
- ½ cup lime juice
- ½ cup finely packed chopped cilantro
- 2 teaspoons ground cumin

Directions: Combine all the vegetables and the garlic and lime in a saucepan and boil, then simmer for 5 minutes, spoon salsa into canning jars, and leave ¼" at the top for the canning process.

Nutrition: Carbs: 30.1g; Fat: 1.1g; Protein: 5.7g; Calories: 132.8

182. Red Pepper Marmalade

Preparation Time: 10 minutes
Canning Time: 15 minutes
Cooking Time: 15 minutes
Servings: 9 pints

Ingredients:
- ¾ cup lemon juice
- 8 large red bell peppers
- ¼ cup orange juice
- ¼ cup red wine vinegar
- 2 cups sugar
- 2 tablespoons tomato paste
- 4 garlic cloves, peeled and chopped
- 1 onion, peeled and finely chopped
- ½ teaspoon salt
- ½ teaspoon cayenne pepper
- 1 teaspoon fresh marjoram, chopped
- 1 teaspoon fresh rosemary, chopped
- Zest of 1 lemon
- Zest of 1 orange

Directions: Half the red bell peppers and remove the core and seeds. Grill the peppers until slightly charred.
Finely chop 6 of the red peppers and slice the remaining 2.
In a saucepan, combine all the ingredients and stir over low heat until all the sugar has dissolved.

Bring the mixture to a boil and simmer for 10 minutes, until the mixture thickens.
Remove the pan from heat and spoon into hot jars, skimming off any foam that is created on top. Wipe down the jars, add the tops and the bands, and process in boiling water for 15 minutes. Remove the jars and cool.

Nutrition: Calories: 449.9; Fat: 7.8g; Fiber: 21.8g; Carbs: 7.7g; Protein: 43.2g

183. Tart Berry Apple Butter

Preparation Time: 10 minutes
Serving: 2 jars

Cooking Time: 2 hours and 30 minutes

Ingredients:
- 6 Granny Smith apples, chopped and cored
- 1 cup fresh cranberries
- ½ cup water
- 1 cinnamon stick
- Raw honey, to taste

Directions: Combine the apples, cranberries, and water; simmer on high for 2–3 hours, stirring periodically to avoid sticking.
Blend the fruit mixture to the desired consistency and pass through a sieve, optional, to get rid of the cranberry skins. Return to the crockpot and add the cinnamon stick. Cook uncovered until you get a batter that's thick to your desire. Taste to gauge the sweetness and add raw honey, if desired.
Scoop into storage jars, cover tightly, and refrigerate or process for canning.

Nutrition: Carbs: 187.9g; Fat: 1.4g; Protein: 2.5g; Calories: 715.9

184. Tropical Fruit Butter

Preparation Time: 15 minutes
Serving: 2 jars

Cooking Time: 30 minutes

Ingredients:
- 1 can crushed pineapple, don't discard the juice
- 5 large ripe bananas, thinly sliced
- ¼ cup fresh coconut, chopped
- ¼ cup freshly squeezed lemon juice
- 1 ½ cups brown sugar

Directions: Bring all of the ingredients to a boil in a heavy-bottomed pan over medium to high heat. Simmer for 20–30 minutes or until the fruit is soft, stirring to ensure it doesn't stick.
Puree the thick batter to desired consistency and scoop into storage jars.
Tightly seal and refrigerate or process for canning.

Nutrition: Carbs: 187.8g; Fat: 1.3g; Protein: 2.5g; Calories: 715.8

185. Caramel Apple Butter

Preparation Time: 10 minutes
Serving: 4 jars

Cooking Time: 4 hours

Ingredients:
- 15 Granny Smith apples— peeled, cored, and cut into small cubes
- 2 cups dark brown sugar
- 2 (250g) packages individually wrapped caramels
- ¼ teaspoon ground cloves
- 2 teaspoons ground cinnamon
- ½ teaspoon ground allspice
- ¼ teaspoon salt

Directions: Place the apples, sugar, salt, and spices in your slow cooker and cook on high until the apples easily break apart, for about 4 hours.
After 2 two hours of cooking time, melt the caramels in your microwave for 30 seconds each and stir into the apple mixture. Puree the apple, if you want it smooth, then pack into prepared jars and refrigerate or process for canning if you want to can.

Nutrition: Carbs: 187.9g; Fat: 1.3g; Protein: 2.5g; Calories: 715.8

186. Pickled Blueberries

Preparation Time: 5 minutes
Serving Sizes: 96

Cooking Time: 15 minutes

Ingredients:
- 3x3" cinnamon sticks
- 1 teaspoon whole cloves
- 1 teaspoon whole allspice berries
- 12 ounces red wine vinegar
- 64 ounces washed fresh blueberries
- 8 ounces white sugar
- 8 ounces brown sugar

Directions: Combine cinnamon, cloves, and berries in a spice bag and place in a large saucepan with the red wine vinegar. Bring the mixture to a simmer for 5 minutes on medium-high heat.
Add blueberries and cook for 5 minutes until heated through. Gently shake the pot as the blueberries cook, but do not stir. Remove the pot from heat and let stand for 12 hours at room temperature.
Pour allspice berries and liquid into a colander over a large bowl. Remove spices in the bag.
Pour berries into sterilized jars according to the canning method and return the liquid to the saucepan. Add sugars and stir, while bringing the mixture to a boil. Boil for 4 minutes until thick.
Spoon the hot liquid over berries in the jars, leaving ½" of space.
Seal the jars according to the canning method.
Nutrition: Calories: 432.7; Fat: 7.9g; Fiber: 1.9g; Carbs: 7.8g

187. Southern Pickled Peaches
Preparation Time: 60 minutes
Serving Sizes: 32
Cooking Time: 24 minutes

Ingredients:
- 32 ounces sugar
- 8 ounces white vinegar
- 8 ounces water
- 1 ounce whole cloves
- 64 ounces blanched and peeled clingstone peaches
- 5x3" cinnamon sticks

Directions: Bring sugar, white vinegar, and 8 ounces of water to a boil in a large pot for 5 minutes.
Press 2 cloves and cinnamon into each peach and add to the liquid in the pan.
Bring the mixture to a boil for 20 minutes until peaches are softened.
Spoon peaches into the jars according to the canning method and seal.
Nutrition: Calories: 232.8; Fat: 7.9g; Fiber: 1.8g; Carbs: 7.9g; Protein: 13.2g

188. Pickled Green Beans
Preparation Time: 10 minutes
Serving Sizes: 8
Cooking Time: 10 minutes

Ingredients:
- 32 ounces rinsed and trimmed green beans
- 4 peeled garlic cloves
- 8 sprigs fresh dill weed
- 2/3 ounce salt
- 20 ounces white vinegar
- 20 ounces water

Directions: Slice the beans to just shorter than the jars so they fit.
Place a steamer insert in a pot and fill with water to just below the steamer. Bring to a boil and place green beans in the steamer insert.
Cook for 3 minutes until tender but firm to the bite. Transfer the beans to a bowl of ice water and drain.
Evenly divide the beans between 4 sterilized jars that are still hot. You can find out how to sterilize by following the canning method.
Place one garlic clove and 2 dill weed sprigs in each jar up against the sides. Pour in 1 teaspoon of salt.
Bring vinegar and water to a boil in a pan and pour over the beans, leaving ¼" of space at the top.
Seal and process according to the canning method.
Nutrition: Calories: 377.9; Fat: 7.9g; Fiber: 1.8g; Carbs: 7.9g; Protein: 6.2g

189. Watermelon Pickles
Preparation Time: 15 minutes
Serving Sizes: 24
Cooking Time: 1 hour and 20 minutes

Ingredients:
- 8 ounces canning salt
- 356 ounces water, divided
- 128 ounces x1" watermelon rind cubes
- 3 cinnamon sticks
- 1 teaspoon whole allspice
- 1 teaspoon whole cloves
- 16 ounces 5% white vinegar

- 24 ounces white sugar
- 12 maraschino cherries, cut in half
- 1 thinly sliced lemon
- 6 canning jars with lids and rings, 1-pint

Directions: Combine canning salt and 128 ounces of water in a large sealable container until salt dissolves. Stir in watermelon rind. Cover the container with a lid or plastic wrap and set aside for 12 hours at room temperature. Drain liquid and rinse rinds thoroughly.
Bring the rest of the water and watermelon rinds to a boil in a large pot. Reduce the heat to medium-low and simmer for 1 hour until rinds are tender. Drain.
In a spice bag or a piece of cheesecloth, combine cinnamon, allspice, and cloves.
Combine white vinegar, white sugar, cherries, and lemon in the pot with the spice bag and stir until sugar is dissolved. Add rinds to the pot and bring the mixture to a boil. Reduce the heat to medium-low and cook for 5–10 minutes until the rinds are transparent. Remove the spice bag and discard.
Sterilize jars according to the canning method. Place one clove per jar and evenly divide pieces of the cinnamon stick amongst the jars. Pack with rinds and pour vinegar into the jars, leaving ¼" of space at the top.
Seal and store according to the canning method.

Nutrition: Calories: 177.9; Fat: 7.9g; Fiber: 1.8g; Carbs: 7.8g; Protein: 6.2g

190. Pickled Radish
Preparation Time: 15 minutes

Serving Sizes: 10

Ingredients:
- 32 ounces warm water
- 6 ounces rice vinegar
- 1 ½ ounces sugar
- 1-ounce salt
- 8 ounces julienned carrots
- 8 ounces julienned white radish (daikon)

Directions: Mix water, rice vinegar, white sugar, and salt in a large bowl and stir until sugar and salt dissolve. Sterilize a jar and add carrots and radish. Pour hot brine over the vegetables, leaving ¼" of space at the top. Seal the jar and store it in the refrigerator for 48–72 hours before using.

Nutrition: Calories: 77.9; Fat: 7.9g; Fiber: 1.9g; Carbs: 7.8g; Protein: 6.2g

191. Pickled Mostaccioli
Preparation Time: 30 minutes
Serving Sizes: 12

Cooking Time: 10 minutes

Ingredients:
- 16 ounces Mostaccioli pasta
- 12 ounces white vinegar
- 12 ounces white sugar
- 1 ounce prepared yellow mustard
- 1 teaspoon garlic powder
- 1 teaspoon salt
- 1 teaspoon black pepper, ground
- 1 teaspoon parsley, dried
- 1 medium quartered onion
- 1 medium diced cucumber

Directions: Boil lightly salted water in a large stockpot and cook pasta in the water for 8–10 minutes until al dente. Drain into a large bowl. Combine the rest of the ingredients in a blender and process for 3 minutes until smooth.
Pour sauce from the blender over the paste and toss to coat. Cover the bowl and chill for 72 hours in the refrigerator. Stir every day until ready to serve.

Nutrition: Calories: 77.9; Fat: 7.9g; Fiber: 1.8g; Carbs: 7.9g; Protein: 6.1g

Conversion Tables

Volume

Imperial	Metric	Imperial	Metric
1 tbsp	15ml	1 pint	570 ml
2 fl oz	55 ml	1 ¼ pints	725 ml
3 fl oz	75 ml	1 ¾ pints	1 liter
5 fl oz (¼ pint)	150 ml	2 pints	1.2 liters
10 fl oz (½ pint)	275 ml	2½ pints	1.5 liters
		4 pints	2.25 liters

Weight

Imperial	Metric	Imperial	Metric	Imperial	Metric
½ oz	10 g	4 oz	110 g	10 oz	275 g
¾ oz	20 g	4½ oz	125 g	12 oz	350 g
1 oz	25 g	5 oz	150 g	1 lb.	450 g
1½ oz	40 g	6 oz	175 g	1 lb. 8 oz	700 g
2 oz	50 g	7 oz	200 g	2 lb.	900 g
2½ oz	60 g	8 oz	225 g	3 lb.	1.35 kg
3 oz	75 g	9 oz	250 g		

Metric cups conversion

Cups	Imperial	Metric
1 cup flour	5oz	150g
1 cup caster or granulated sugar	8oz	225g
1 cup soft brown sugar	6oz	175g
1 cup soft butter/margarine	8oz	225g
1 cup sultanas/raisins	7oz	200g
1 cup currants	5oz	150g
1 cup ground almonds	4oz	110g
1 cup oats	4oz	110g
1 cup golden syrup/honey	12oz	350g
1 cup uncooked rice	7oz	200g
1 cup grated cheese	4oz	110g
1 stick butter	4oz	110g
¼ cup liquid (water, milk, oil etc.)	4 tablespoons	60ml
½ cup liquid (water, milk, oil etc.)	¼ pint	125ml
1 cup liquid (water, milk, oil etc.)	½ pint	250ml

Oven temperatures

Gas Mark	Fahrenheit	Celsius	Gas Mark	Fahrenheit	Celsius
1/4	225	110	4	350	180
1/2	250	130	5	375	190
1	275	140	6	400	200
2	300	150	7	425	220
3	325	170	8	450	230
			9	475	240

Made in United States
Troutdale, OR
07/10/2023